Lowfat Korean Cooking
by Susan Kim

This traditional table and dishes are set for a meal for one person. Korean women have been serving meals this way for about 5,000 years.

Published by:

SUSAN KIM'S COOKBOOKS
P.O. Box 34, Auburn, CA 95604-0034
Phone: (916) 823-8461

Lowfat Korean Cooking

by Susan Kim

Original Copyright © 1995 by Susan Kim

Second Printing May 1997

First Printing May 1995

ISBN 0-9656125-9-7

EAN 978-0-9656125-9-3

Library of Congress Catalog Card Number: 95-195916

Library of Congress Cataloging in Publication Data

Kim, Susan

Lowfat Korean Cooking/by Susan Kim

Auburn, CA: Susan Kim's Cookbooks, [c1995]

126 p.: col. ill.; 29 cm.

Printed in the United States of America

Printing by: Lectramedia - Nevada City, California (530) 478-8300

I would like to dedicate this cookbook to my son, Thomas Wilson, and my daughter, Jennifer Wilson, so they may have a better life than I have experienced . . . because now I have started to overcome my disabilities from being a victim of a crime.

I created and Americanized these recipes for everyone to enjoy.

Susan Kim

ACKNOWLEDGMENTS

Our grateful appreciation to the following individuals for their help and encouragement throughout the many months it took to finish this book:

ANNE HOUSE, Dictation

GLORIA WOLLACE, Dictation

JENNIFER WILSON, Dictation, Proofreading

JAN CLEMENT, Typing, Dictation

JUDYANNE HUTCHISON, Printing Support

THOMAS WILSON, Editorial Director, Dictation, Typing, Proofreading,

Photography (*Muchim, Kim Chee, Chop Chee, Solgulge Jung Jo Dum*)

LEE WHITING, Photography (*Cover, Title, Author, Chighe*)

MARIA L. RUBALCAVA, Typesetting

DOREEN WOOD, Typesetting

KAE BOON KIM & FAMILY, Financial Support

ABOUT THE AUTHOR . . . .

Susan Kim was born in Pusan, Korea. She has been cooking Korean Cuisine for the past 32 years. Her creations of unique and tasty foods have delighted thousands of people.

Recipes throughout this book range from traditional Korean cooking, using recipes that have been in the Kim family for over five generations, to cooking of the 90's.

Korean food is healthy, low-fat, and inexpensive. It can be served for casual dinners or elegant affairs.

TABLE OF CONTENTS

Beverages

KOREAN RICE PUNCH

You will have 2-3 quarts of malt flour sediment remaining after preparing this recipe. The sediment can be used in cooking "Hot Bean Paste Sauce" or it may be discarded.

2   cups rice
1   pound malt flour
5-6 quarts water, divided

Cook rice and set aside. (See Steamed Rice recipe on page 3.)

In large bowl, soak malt flour in 1 quart of cold water for 1 hour. Separate malt from husks: squeeze husks, and soak in water, remove, strain water and set aside. Squeeze husks second time in 2 quarts fresh water, remove; strain water and add to that already set aside. Squeeze husks third time in 2 additional quarts fresh water. Discard husks. Strain water and add to water which has been processed. You will have 5-6 quarts water which will be whitish in color. Set malt flour water aside until clear water rises to top, about 2 hours.

Add 3 quarts clear malt-flour water to cooked rice in large pan or in rice cooker. Stir and cover. Turn heat to very low. Stirring occasionally, keep mixture warm until 30-50 rice grains rises to surface of water-in about 3 1/2 hours.

Add mixture to 1 gallon water, in large pot. Boil uncovered at high temperature for 1/2 hour. Cool and refrigerate. Before serving, add sugar to taste.

HOT APPLE-ORANGE TEA

2   apples
2   peels from fresh oranges, well washed
1   cup sugar
1   tablespoon whole allspice
2   quarts water

Wash, quarter, and core apples.

Combine all ingredients in a large pot. Bring to a boil and cook under low heat for 20 minutes. Apple pieces will be soft but not broken.

Immediately after removing from heat, take out apple quarters. (These make a excellent dessert when served cold).

Strain punch and discard orange peels and allspice. Return punch to pan, and serve hot. Yields 8 1/2 cups.

PUMPKIN TEA

1 pumpkin (3-7 lbs.)
2 pounds ginger
2 ounces cinnamon sticks

Cut pumpkin into 4 pieces and remove all seeds. Peel skin off ginger and wash well. Slice ginger into small pieces. Boil pumpkin, ginger and cinnamon in 8 quarts of water on high heat for a half hour. Cook on low heat for two and a half hours. Remove all ingredients and strain through a fine strainer. Refrigerate after drinking. Add sugar to taste.

APPLE AND LEMON TEA

2 quarts water
1 pound ginger root
2 green apples
1 lemon peel

Peel ginger root, scraping with knife. Cut into 1/8 inch slices. Quarter and peel apples. Mix slices, peelings, and apples with 2 quarts water, and boil on low temperature for 1/2 hour. Separate root, apples, and lemon peelings from tea. Serve.

GINGER ROOT TEA

** *After tea is gone, roots and peels may be used over again.*

1/2 pound ginger root
2 quarts water
5 tangerine peels

Peel ginger, scraping with knife. Slice in 1/8 inch slices. Add tangerine peels. Boil for 1/2 hour in 2 quarts water. Separate roots and peels from tea. Serve tea.

GINGER-PERSIMMON PUNCH

4 quarts water
2 cups fresh ginger roots
2 ounces cinnamon sticks
7 dried persimmons (usually at Asian market)
1/2 cup pine nuts
2 cups sugar (more if desired)

Put water into a large pot. Prepare the ginger root. Clean outer surface of root; cut into 1/2 inch pieces. Add to pot, ginger and cinnamon sticks. Boil rapidly for a 1/2 hour. Cook on low heat for 2 and 1/2 hours.

While the ginger and cinnamon boil, prepare the persimmons. Boil 6 cups of water and the persimmons; low boil for 1/2 hour, and drain into a separate pan. Save juice and persimmons separately. Set aside. Refrigerate persimmons.

When done, strain the ginger and cinnamon out. Use a fine strainer to make the punch as clear as possible. Discard ginger and cinnamon sticks. Add the sugar and persimmon juice. Refrigerate until very cold. Punch may be prepared a day ahead. Put in a punch bowl. Add the cold persimmons and the pine nuts. Serve.

Rice Dishes

NOTE: Most Koreans use short grain rice. All types of rice can be used.

STEAMED SHORT GRAIN RICE

1 **cup short grain rice**
1 **cup water**

Put rice into a 2 quart pan or larger. Wash rice by kneading it against the bottom of the pan. Rinse rice until the water is clear. Cover rice with water and soak for 1/2 hour. Drain water and then add 1 cup of water to 1 cup of rice. Boil on high for 5 minutes. When it starts boiling remove cover and observe when the water recedes and boil holes appear at top, and then turn heat as low as possible. Then replace cover and cook on low heat for 5 minutes. Turn off heat and let set for 10 minutes. Ready to Serve.

TRADITIONAL KOREAN CLAY POT RICE

1 **cup short grain rice**
1 **cup water**
   Clay pot, about 5" in diameter by 3" deep
   (Special pot for cooking on stove burner – usually available at Korean market.)

Rinse rice well. Cover with water and soak for 1/2 hour. Drain and put rice in clay pot and add the one cup of water. Put pot on stove gas burner and boil fast for 5 minutes. When it starts boiling remove cover and observe when the water recedes and boil holes appear at top, and then turn flame as low as possible. Then replace cover and slow heat for 5 minutes. Turn off burner and let set for 10 minutes more. Pot will be hot. Use caution. Now it is ready. Adjust procedure for your appliance. An electric stove will take longer to start the boil. Ready to Serve.

STEAMED RICE WITH SOYBEANS AND PORK

1 pound pork, chopped
1/8 cup sesame oil
2 pounds soybean bean sprouts
2 cups rice
1/2 yellow onion
2 cups water
2 green onions, minced
1 1/2 cups soy sauce
1 tablespoon sesame oil
1 tablespoon sesame seeds (roasted)
1 tablespoon hot chili pepper powder
1/2 teaspoon garlic powder
1/4 teaspoon sugar

Chop pork into 1/4 inch pieces. Wash bean sprouts. Wash 2 cups short grain rice, and soak for 1/2 hour. Drain.

Chop yellow onion and mix with pork. Saute in 1/8 cup sesame oil, for 5 minutes. Spread bean sprouts on top of sauted meat. Take rice and put on top of bean sprouts. Add 2 cups water to pan. Cook for 10 more minutes on low temperature. When water is gone and bubbles come up, turn heat off and let rice mixture sit for 10 minutes. Lightly mix the contents of the pan.

Mix green onions, soy sauce, 1 tablespoon sesame oil, sesame seeds, hot chili pepper powder, garlic powder and sugar together in a bowl. Keep separate when served.

To eat put desired amount of sauce on rice mixture. Serves 2-3 people.

STEAMED RICE WITH SOYBEAN BEAN SPROUTS

2 pounds soybean bean sprouts
2 cups rice
2 cups water
2 green onions, minced
1 1/2 cups soy sauce
1 tablespoon sesame oil
1 tablespoon sesame seeds (roasted)
1 tablespoon hot chili pepper powder
1/2 teaspoon garlic powder
1/4 teaspoon sugar

Wash bean sprouts. Wash 2 cups short grain rice and soak for 1/2 hour. Drain. Put bean sprouts in pan and top with 2 cups rice. Pour 2 cups water into pan and cook for 10 minutes, on low temperature.

When water is gone and bubbles come up, turn the heat low, and cook for 5 minutes. Turn off heat and let sit for 10 minutes. Mix contents of pan together, and set aside.

Mix remaining ingredients for the sauce in a bowl. Keep separate to serve.

When ready to eat, put desired amount of sauce on rice mixture. Serves 2-3 people.

STEAMED RICE WITH RADISHES

2   cups radish (daikon)
2   cups rice
2   cups water
2   green onions, minced
1 1/2 cups soy sauce
1   tablespoon sesame oil
1   tablespoon sesame seeds (roasted)
1   tablespoon hot chili pepper powder
1/2 teaspoon garlic powder
1/4 teaspoon sugar

Cut radish like thin french fries. Wash 2 cups rice and soak for 1/2 hour. Drain.

Put radishes in pan and top with 2 cups rice. Pour 2 cups water into pan and cook for 10 minutes, on high temperature. When water is gone and bubbles come up, turn the heat low and cook for 5 more minutes. Then turn off heat and let sit for 10 minutes. Then mix contents of pan together. Set aside.

Mix the remaining ingredients for the sauce in a bowl. Keep separate to serve.

When ready to eat, put desired amount of sauce on rice mixture. Serves 2-3 people.

KIM'S FRIED RICE (KOREAN STYLE)

2   cups rice
2   carrots (chopped into pea size pieces)
2   yellow onions (cut into pea size pieces)
1   8 ounce package frozen peas
1   tablespoon sesame oil
3   green onions (with tops)
1   pound precooked ham
2   cups water
     Frying oil
     Garlic salt (to taste)

Put rice into a 3 quart pan. Wash rice by kneading it against the bottom of the pan. Rinse rice until water is clear. Drain water and pour in 2 cups of water. Bring to a boil and reduce heat to simmer. Cover and simmer for 20 minutes.

Saute carrots for 5 minutes. Saute onions and peas for 2 minutes. Mince ham and saute for 2 minutes. Mix rice with carrots, yellow onion, ham and peas. Add minced green onions, sesame seed oil, and garlic salt. Mix well.

Ready to Serve.

Notes

Salads

SPINACH SALAD

3 bundles spinach
1-3 jalapeno peppers
5 green onions, with tops
1 cup soy sauce
2 tablespoons sesame seeds (roasted)
1 teaspoon hot red pepper powder
1 teaspoon garlic powder
1 tablespoon sugar
1/4 teaspoon black pepper

Cut off root portion of spinach. Wash well, and drain in colander for at least 10 minutes to remove excess water. Slice peppers lengthwise in four pieces; remove seeds and mince. Mince green onions.

Put soy sauce in a medium bowl. Add jalapeno pepper(s), onions, seeds, red pepper, garlic powder, sugar, and black pepper.

Place about 1/5 of the spinach in a large bowl. Sprinkle 1/5 of the soy sauce mixture over the spinach. Continue to alternate spinach and sauce until you have 5 or 6 layers. Let rest for at least 20 minutes. Carefully turn salad over. Let stand another 20 minutes before serving. Serves 5-6 people.

ASPARAGUS SALAD

1 bundle (1 lb.) fresh asparagus
2 green onions with tops
1 tablespoon sesame oil
1 tablespoon sesame seeds (roasted)
1/8 teaspoon black pepper
1 teaspoon garlic powder
1 teaspoon red pepper powder (optional)

Rinse and trim asparagus. Cut the long spears in half lengthwise and boil rapidly for 5 minutes. Drain and rinse with cool water. Slice green onions thin about 1/16 inch. Mix all ingredients except asparagus in a bowl. Then place asparagus in a serving bowl and put dressing on top and mix in well. Usually served with rice.

MINIATURE SQUID SALAD

3 cups miniature squid
1 English cucumber, slice 1/4-inch thick
5 green onions, 2 inches long
1 red hot pepper, without seeds, cut like french fries
5 jalapeno peppers, without seeds, cut like french fries
1 tablespoon red pepper powder
1 tablespoon hot paste
1 tablespoon sesame seeds (roasted)
1/3 cup white vinegar
1 tablespoon sugar
1 teaspoon chopped garlic
1 tablespoon soy sauce
1/4 teaspoon black pepper

Clean squid and wash. Boil 5 cups water. Add squid and boil for 5 minutes. Cut bottoms off of green onions and wash. Then cut into 2-inch long pieces. Place squid, cucumber, onions, red pepper, and jalapeno peppers in a large bowl. Mix remaining ingredients in another bowl. Pour over squid and vegetables. Mix. Serve with rice.

STINGRAY FISH SALAD

2 cups jalapeno peppers
2 cups green onions
1 tablespoon crushed fresh garlic
4 cups stingray fish
3 cups water
1 cup white vinegar
1/4 cup sesame seeds (roasted)
1/4 cup sugar
1/4 cup hot red pepper powder
1/2 cup hot red bean paste

Cut fish into 1 inch square pieces. Wash thoroughly. Mix water and 1/2 cup of vinegar together. Pour on to fish. Let set for 20 minutes. Drain and wash the fish. Squeeze moisture out of the fish. Add pepper powder. Mix together. Add remaining ingredients. Mix well and serve.

TAKUWAN SALAD

12.3 ounces Takuwan (pickled radish)
2   green onions, with tops
1   tablespoon sesame oil
2   teaspoons sesame seeds (roasted)
1   tablespoon hot red bean paste
1   teaspoon garlic powder
1   teaspoon hot red pepper powder
1   teaspoon sugar (optional)

Cut Takuwan lengthwise and slice into 1/4 inch pieces. Mince onions. Combine all ingredients and mix well. Serve.

ACORN SALAD

2   quarts acorn gelatin*
1/4   cup soy sauce
1   tablespoon sesame oil
2   tablespoons sesame seeds (roasted)
2   green onions with tops
1   tablespoon red pepper powder
1   teaspoon black pepper
1/4   teaspoon sugar (optional)
1   teaspoon garlic powder

Cut acorn gelatin into pieces about 1/2 inch by 2 inches. Put in a bowl and set aside. Chop onions fine.

Mix in a small bowl: soy sauce, sesame oil, chopped onions, sesame seeds, red pepper, black pepper, garlic and sugar. Stir well. With acorn gelatin in the serving bowl pour sauce over it. Stir in sauce. If desired can be warmed for 2 minutes in the microwave. May also be served with sauce in separate bowl allowing the pieces of gelatin to be dipped individually as eaten. Usually served with rice.

Usually available at Asian Markets

KOSHER DILL PICKLE SALAD

3   medium (4 inch) kosher dill pickles
1   green onion (with top)
1/4   teaspoon garlic powder
1   teaspoon sesame seeds (roasted)
1/4   teaspoon hot red pepper powder
1   cup water
1   tablespoon rice vinegar
1/2   teaspoon sugar

Cut pickles across into 1/3 inch pieces and place in a bowl. Mince the onion. Add all ingredients to the pickles. Stir well. This salad is best when it is served with short grain rice. Serves 5-6 People.

PLAIN SEAWEED SALAD (STEMS)

1-10 ounce package salted seaweed stems*
2   green onions with tops
1   tablespoon sesame seeds (roasted)
1   teaspoon garlic powder
2   tablespoons rice vinegar
1/8   teaspoon black pepper powder
1/4   teaspoon soy sauce
1   teaspoon sugar

Soak seaweed in a bowl for one hour. Then wash thoroughly to remove salt. Cut with kitchen shears into bite-size pieces. Slice onions into thin slices about 1/16 inch. Put all ingredients for dressing (all except sea-weed) in a bowl and mix well. Place prepared seaweed in a bowl and mix well. Place prepared seaweed in a serving bowl and place the pre-pared dressing on top and mix in well. Usually served with rice.

Usually available at Asian Markets

SEAWEED SALAD (WITH PICKLED RADISHES)

This recipe is prepared in two parts. The radish must be pickled at least 2 and 1/2 hours before adding it to the salad.

For pickling radish:

1 fresh medium white radish (daikon)
2 tablespoons salt
2 quarts water
1 cup vinegar
1 cup sugar

Slice radish in 1/3 inch pieces. In large bowl, mix in salt, and let stand for a 1/2 hour. Wash well. Return to bowl, add water, vinegar, and sugar. Let stand for at least 2 hours. Serve.

For Seaweed Salad:

10 ounces salted seaweed or 1-2 ounces dried seaweed
5 green onions, with tops
1 quart pickled radish (see recipe above)
2 tablespoons sesame seeds (roasted)
2 tablespoons hot red bean paste, or to taste
1 tablespoon garlic powder or 3 cloves fresh garlic
2 tablespoons vinegar, or to taste
1 teaspoon soy sauce
1 teaspoon salt
1 teaspoon black pepper
Sugar to taste (optional)

Soak seaweed for 1/2 hour. Wash well and cut into large pieces. Mince green onions. Combine all ingredients and mix well. Serve.

VEGETARIAN SALAD

4 carrots
2 yellow onions
2 red bell peppers
2 bundles green onions
2 bundles spinach
1 tablespoon sesame seeds (roasted)
1 teaspoon black pepper
1/4 teaspoon garlic powder
1 teaspoon salt
1 teaspoon sesame oil
1 teaspoon sugar
12 ounce package Dang Myun noodles (sweet potato noodles or bean thread)

(Boil all items separately)

Cut carrots into 2 inch long slivers and boil in 8 cups of water for 10 minutes. Cut green onions in 2 inch long pieces and boil in 8 cups of water for 10 minutes. Cut bell peppers into lengthwise slivers and boil in 8 cups of water for 10 minutes. Cut roots off spinach and boil in 8 cups of water for 10 minutes.

After boiling items rinse in cold water and let set. Cut yellow onions into 2 inch pieces and saute on low heat for about 3 minutes. Bring 8 cups of water to a boil and add noodles. Cook noodles in boiling water for 5 minutes. Turn off heat and let set for 10 minutes. Rinse noodles in cold water. Mix vegetables and noodles together. Serves 9-10 People.

HOT FLAVORED WATERCRESS SALAD

8   cups watercress
2   tablespoons fish sauce
1   tablespoon hot pepper powder
1/2 teaspoon sugar
1   tablespoon sesame seeds (roasted)
1/4 teaspoon black pepper
1/2 teaspoon garlic powder
3   green onions, chopped
2   jalapeno peppers, chopped

Optional:
1/2 cup pine nuts

Mix all ingredients except watercress, jalapeno peppers and green onions in a bowl. Wash watercress well to make sure clean. Set aside.

Wash green onions and cut roots off. Chop. Quarter jalapeno peppers, remove seeds and chop thin. Add watercress, green onions and peppers to sauce and mix. Serve.

WATERCRESS SALAD

1/4 teaspoon black pepper
1/2 teaspoon sesame oil
1   tablespoon sesame seeds (roasted)
1/2 teaspoon soy sauce
1   tablespoon hot paste
1/2 teaspoon sugar
2   green onions, chopped
2   cups cooked watercress

Wash green onions and cut roots off. Chop. Mix remaining ingredients except watercress in a bowl. Add green onions and watercress and mix. Serve.

HOT FLAVORED CUCUMBER AND CABBAGE SALAD

2   cups cabbage
1/3 cup white vinegar
3   tablespoons hot paste
1   tablespoon sugar
1/2 teaspoon worcestershire sauce
1/2 teaspoon sesame seeds (roasted)
1/4 teaspoon black pepper
5   green onions, 1-inch long pieces
1/2 English cucumber, sliced 1/4-inch thick
1   teaspoon salt

Mix all ingredients except cabbage, green onions and cucumber in a bowl. Cut cabbage in fourths and slice thinly. Set aside. Wash green onions and cut off roots. Chop. Slice English cucumber into 1/4-inch thick slices. Mix cabbage, green onions and cucumber with sauce. Serve.

HOT FLAVORED CUCUMBER SALAD

1   English cucumber
1   tablespoon red pepper powder
3   tablespoons hot paste
1/3 cup sugar
1/2 teaspoon chopped garlic
1/2 cup vinegar
5   green onions chopped
1   tablespoon sesame seeds (roasted)

Cut bottoms off of green onions and wash. Then chop. Mix red pepper powder, hot paste, sugar, garlic, vinegar and green onions in a bowl. Slice cucumber into 1/4-inch thick slices. Put in a large bowl and add sesame seeds. Add sauce and mix. Serve.

CABBAGE SALAD

1	green onion, chopped
1	tablespoon soy sauce
1/2	medium cabbage
1	teaspoon sesame oil
1	teaspoon garlic powder
1	tablespoon sesame seeds (roasted)
1/4	teaspoon black pepper

Optional:

1	teaspoon hot pepper powder

Cut cabbage in half. Wash well. In 5 cups water cook for 5 minutes, stirring occasionally. Take out and wash with cold water. Squeeze dry. Cut into bite-size pieces, and put in a bowl. Add the rest of the ingredients in the bowl. Add the remaining ingredients to the bowl and mix. Add salt to taste. Ready to serve.

NAPA CABBAGE SALAD

1	green onion, chopped
1	tablespoon soy sauce
1	medium napa cabbage
1	teaspoon sesame oil
1	teaspoon garlic powder
1	tablespoon sesame seeds (roasted)
1/4	teaspoon black pepper

Optional:

1	teaspoon hot pepper powder

Cut cabbage in half. Wash well. In 5 cups water cook for 5 minutes, stirring occasionally. Take out and wash with cold water. Squeeze dry. Cut into bite-size pieces. Add remaining ingredients to the bowl and mix. Add salt to taste. Ready to serve.

HOT FLAVORED SWISS CHARD SALAD

1	tablespoon sesame seeds (roasted)
1	teaspoon garlic, chopped
2	green onions, chopped
3	jalapeno peppers, chopped
1/4	teaspoon black pepper
1	tablespoon hot paste
1	tablespoon hot pepper powder
1	teaspoon sesame oil
1	tablespoon soy sauce
1	bundle Swiss chard

Wash Swiss chard. Boil 5 cups water. Add chard and cook for 10 minutes. When done, chop. Squeeze chard dry. Then mix all ingredients in a bowl. Serve with rice.

HOT FLAVORED CABBAGE SALAD

3	cups cabbage
1	tablespoon hot pepper powder
1	tablespoon sesame oil
1/2	teaspoon garlic powder
1	tablespoon sesame seeds (roasted)
1/4	teaspoon black pepper
1/2	teaspoon sugar
2	tablespoons soy sauce
3	green onions, chopped
1/2	teaspoon salt
2	jalapeno peppers, chopped

Mix all ingredients except cabbage, jalapeno peppers and green onions, in a bowl. Wash green onions, cut off roots and then chop. Wash cabbage. Cut in fourths and slice thin. Quarter jalapeno peppers, remove seeds and then chop. Add peppers, cabbage and green onions to sauce and mix. Serve.

HOT FLAVORED SOYBEAN SPROUT SALAD

1   pound soybean sprouts
1   tablespoon hot paste
1   tablespoon soy sauce
1   teaspoon chopped garlic
1   teaspoon sesame oil
1   tablespoon crushed sesame seeds (roasted)
3   green onions
2   jalapeno peppers, chopped

Combine all ingredients in large bowl. Season with salt to taste if desired. Serve.

HOT FLAVORED SOYBEAN SPROUT WITH STARCH NOODLE SALAD

6   ounces oriental style starch noodles
1   pound soybean sprouts
1   bunch spinach, rinsed well
1   teaspoon hot paste
1   tablespoon crushed sesame seeds (roasted)
1   teaspoon sesame oil
1   teaspoon soy sauce
1   teaspoon chopped garlic
1   tablespoon red pepper powder
5   green onions, minced

Put noodles into boiling water and set aside for 10 minutes. Cook bean sprouts in 5 cups water for 10 minutes. Chop spinach leaves and boil for 2 minutes. Rinse with cold water and drain. Press to remove all excess water. Combine all ingredients in medium size bowl. Serve with rice.

MUNGBEAN SPROUT SALAD

1   tablespoon soy sauce
1   pound mung bean sprouts
1   teaspoon sesame oil
1   green onion, chopped
1   teaspoon garlic powder
1   tablespoon sesame seeds (roasted)
1/4   teaspoon black pepper

Optional:

1   teaspoon hot pepper powder

Wash sprouts. Cook in 5 cups water for 5 minutes stirring occasionally. Take out and wash with cold water. Squeeze dry. Cut into bite-size pieces. Add the remaining ingredients to the bowl and mix. Add salt to taste. Ready to serve.

HOT FLAVORED LEEK SALAD

2   whole leeks
1   cup hot paste
1   green onion, chopped
1/8   cup vinegar
1/8   cup sugar

Cut each leek into four sections. Wash well. Boil in 5 cups water for 5 minutes, stirring occasionally. Strain, but don't rinse. Slice into 2-inch long pieces. Combine remaining ingredients with leeks. Ready to serve.

DRIED DAIKON SALAD (MUCHIM)

(See color photograph.)

2   cups soy sauce
5   green onions
4   cups dried daikon radish*
1   tablespoon crushed garlic
3   tablespoons sesame seeds (roasted)
5   tablespoons hot red pepper powder
2   tablespoons sugar
1   tablespoon sesame oil
2   green jalapeno peppers

Rinse radish twice and allow to drain. Mix radish with soy sauce and set aside for one hour at room temperature. Stir after one hour. Cut green onions into 2 inch pieces. Quarter and remove seeds from jalapeno peppers. Combine radish, green onions, garlic, sesame seeds, red pepper, sugar, sesame seed oil, and jalapenos. Can be stored in the refrigerator up to one month before it expires.

Usually available at Asian markets.

RED LEAF LETTUCE SALAD

1/3   cup soy sauce
1/8   cup vinegar
1   tablespoon crushed sesame seeds (roasted)
2   green onions, chopped
1/2   teaspoon sugar
1/4   teaspoon crushed garlic
1   red lettuce head, whole

Remove stem of red lettuce. Wash and dry off water. Shred. Put in a bowl. Mix remaining ingredients and pour over top of lettuce. Let sit for 1/2 hour. Turn over and let sit for another 1/2 hour. Ready to serve.

HOT FLAVORED RADISH SALAD

3   green onions, chopped
1   tablespoon sesame seeds (roasted)
1/2   teaspoon garlic powder
3   teaspoons soy sauce
1/2   teaspoon black pepper
1/2   teaspoon sugar
3   teaspoons vinegar
1   tablespoon hot pepper powder
1   medium radish (daikon), cut like thin french fries
1/4   teaspoon salt

Slice radish like thin french fries. Mix with remaining ingredients in a bowl. Serve.

RADISH SALAD

1   tablespoon worcestershire sauce
2   tablespoons sesame seeds (roasted)
2   tablespoons soy sauce
1   tablespoon sesame oil
1/2   teaspoon garlic powder
3   green onions, chopped
1   medium radish (daikon), cut like thin french fries
1/2   teaspoon black pepper
1/2   teaspoon sugar

Optional:
1   tablespoon hot pepper powder

Slice radish like thin french fries. Mix with remaining ingredients in a bowl. Serve.

MUCHIM
(Dried Diakon Salad)

RADISH SALAD WITH RAW OYSTERS

16 ounces oyster, raw
1 medium white radish, shredded
1 cup red pepper powder
1/2 cup crushed sesame seeds (roasted)
1 tablespoon chopped garlic
5 green onions, 1-inch long
5 jalapeno peppers, sliced lengthwise
1 teaspoon minced ginger
2 tablespoons soy sauce
1 tablespoon sesame oil
1 tablespoon sugar
1 teaspoon salt
1/2 teaspoon black pepper

Combine all ingredients in large bowl. Mix well. Season to taste. Serve.

HOT FLAVORED KIMCHEE NOODLE SALAD

6 ounces Japanese vermicelli noodles
2 cups chopped kimchee
1/2 teaspoon sesame oil
1 tablespoon sesame seeds (roasted)
2 green onions, chopped
1 teaspoon white sugar

Optional:
1/2 teaspoon hot paste

Mix all ingredients except noodles in a bowl. Set aside. Put noodles in boiling water and boil for a few minutes. Drain noodles.

Mix noodles with kimchee. Ready to serve. Serves 2 people.

SESAME LEAF SALAD

1 green onion, chopped
1 tablespoon soy sauce
3 bundles sesame leaves
1 teaspoon sesame oil
1 teaspoon sugar
1 teaspoon garlic powder
1 tablespoon sesame seeds (roasted)
1/4 teaspoon black pepper

Optional:
1 teaspoon hot red pepper powder

Prepare 5 cups boiling water and stir in all the leaves. Boil leaves for 5 minutes. Rinse with cold water and squeeze all the water out. Place leaves in large bowl. Mix the remaining ingredients in a small bowl. Combine sauce with sesame leaves and mix. Serve with rice.

KOREAN RADISH SALAD

1 Korean radish (daikon)
2 green onions, including tops
1/4 cup white vinegar
1/4 cup white sugar
1/2 teaspoon garlic salt

Wash and peel radish. Slice into very thin slices. Mince green onions. Place them in a glass bowl. Mix vinegar, sugar, and garlic salt together. Add radishes and green onions.

Cover and let sit for about 5 hours in the refrigerator before serving.

PEPPERLEAVES SALAD

Before making salad, prepare pickled pepperleaves . . .

To prepare pickled pepperleaves, take a whole pepper plant. Wash well, removing all dirt. Separate stems, leaves and peppers. Lay a portion of pepperleaves and sprinkle with salt. Add another layer of leaves and sprinkle with salt. Repeat process until all leaves are layered.

Cover bowl and let sit for 3 hours. Turn mixture in bowl. Let sit for 3 more hours, turn, sit 3 more hours, and turn again. Remove mixture from bowl and place in jar, leaving a 1-inch space at the top. Seal tightly and refrigerate. May be kept for up to one year.

2	cups pepperleaves
1	tablespoon sesame seeds (roasted)
1	teaspoon garlic
1	teaspoon red pepper powder
1/2	teaspoon sugar
1/2	teaspoon sesame oil
3	green onion, minced
2	jalapeno peppers, minced
	pepperleave pickles

Wash and squeeze pepperleaves. Chop onions. Mix all ingredients in a bowl. Ready to serve.

TURNIP MISO SALAD

1	tablespoon sesame seeds (roasted)
1	teaspoon sesame oil
1/4	teaspoon black pepper
2	teaspoons soybean paste
2	green onions, chopped
3	cups turnip tops
1/2	teaspoon garlic powder
1/4	teaspoon salt
1	teaspoon red pepper powder

Boil 6 cups water. Add 2 bundles of turnip and cook for 10 minutes. Wash well. Soak for 2 days, changing water once a day.

Cut into bite-size pieces. Squeeze water out, and then mix with all ingredients in a bowl. Serve.

CUCUMBER SALAD

3	English cucumbers
2	green onions, including tops
1/4	cup white vinegar
1/4	cup white sugar
1/2	teaspoon garlic salt

Wash and peel cucumbers. Cut into thin slices. Wash and mince green onions. Place them in a glass bowl. Mix vinegar, sugar, and garlic salt together with the cucumbers and green onions. Cover and let sit for about 5 hours in the refrigerator before serving.

Soups

CORNISH HEN SOUP

1   Cornish hen
1/8   teaspoon salt
1/3   cup rice
5   cloves garlic
3   dried red dates
3   dried chestnuts
1   quart water

Wash, clean, and drain Cornish hen. Sprinkle salt in cavity. Wash rice well, drain, and put in cavity. Add whole garlic, dates, and chestnuts. Sew cavity closed.

Bring water to a boil and cook for 1 hour. Ready to Serve.

CHICKEN CHAYOTE SOUP

1   Chayote squash
3   green onions
1   tablespoon crushed garlic
2   chicken thighs, skinless
5   cups water
1   jalapeno pepper
1/4   teaspoon salt

Boil chicken thighs in two cups of water for thirty minutes. Cut green onions into two inch pieces. Peel and cut chayote squash into one inch squares. Quarter and deseed the jalapeno pepper. Add crushed garlic, onions, pepper and squash to the boiling water. Add salt, 3 cups of water and continue boiling for thirty more minutes. Ready to Serve.

CHICKEN-BROCCOLI EGGDROP SOUP

1 tablespoon flour
8 cups chicken broth
3 cups broccoli
5 asparagus, 1-inch long
1/2 yellow onion, chopped
5 green onions, 1-inch long
1/2 pound fresh mushrooms, sliced
4 boneless chicken thighs
1/2 teaspoon garlic powder
1 teaspoon salt
2 eggs
1/2 cup water
1/4 teaspoon black pepper

Cut broccoli into bite-size pieces. Boil broccoli in 5 cups water for 5 minutes. Rinse with cold water. Set aside.

Cut onions, mushrooms, asparagus and chicken thighs. Boil chicken in 15 cups water for 10 minutes. Save 8 cups of chicken broth.

Boil 8 cups of chicken broth. Add chicken, onions, mushrooms, broccoli and seasonings. Mix 1/2 cup water and 1 tablespoon flour together. Add to soup for thickening. Cook for 10 minutes.

Beat eggs together. When soup is hot, slowly pour in egg. Don't mix. When egg is firm, stir. Serve with rice. Serves 5 people.

CHICKEN AND SEAWEED SOUP

History: Koreans encourage pregnant women to consume seaweed soup because it provides them with calcium and iron which they generally lack during pregnancy and after child birth.

1 medium chicken
10 ounce package salted seaweed or dried seaweed
5 quarts water
1 tablespoon garlic salt (optional)

Clean chicken. Remove skin and boil for one hour and 30 minutes in 4 quarts of water. Add well washed seaweed, 1 quart of water and cook on high for 1 hour. Mix well and serve.

Optional: add salt and black pepper to taste.

CHICKEN AND RICE SOUP

2 quarts water
1/2 chicken
1/8 teaspoon garlic powder
1/2 teaspoon salt
1-2 ginseng roots (optional)

Remove skin and fat from chicken and wash well. Bring 2 quarts water to a boil. Add chicken. Cover and simmer for a 1/2 hour or until chicken is tender. Remove from water and strip meat from bones. Set meat aside.

Soak rice for 20 minutes in cold water to cover. Drain. Measure 5 cups of chicken stock, adding water if necessary. Add ginseng roots, if desired. Boil stock rapidly for 10 minutes. Add rice. Continue to boil rapidly for approximately 10 minutes, checking for desired consistency of rice. Stir in chicken, garlic powder, and salt. Serve.

HOMEMADE CHICKEN NOODLE SOUP

2   quarts water
2   cups flour
1/2 teaspoon salt
1   cup cold water
1/2 chicken
3   zucchini
3   green onions, chopped
1   teaspoon garlic, chopped

Peel skin off chicken. Boil chicken in 2 quarts water, for 1/2 hour. Save water. Take chicken out and tear meat off. Set aside.

Cut zucchini like small french fries, and then fry them in 1 tablespoon sesame oil. Set aside. Boil garlic and salt in chicken stock for 20 minutes. Fry green onions. Set aside.

Mix flour and salt in a bowl. Gradually add 1 cup water. Roll out flat, about 10 inches wide. Put flour on top, and roll out. Cut thin slices off. Sprinkle with flour so they don't sick. Boil in chicken broth for 10 minutes.

Add chicken and onions. Cook for 5 minutes.

When ready to eat, put zucchini in a bowl and top with chicken soup.

HOT FLAVORED FERN SOUP (WITH CHICKEN)

2   quarts water
1/2 chicken
4   cups ferns (go-sa-de)
1   medium onion
3   bunches green onions with tops
2   cloves garlic
1/4 cup cayenne pepper (or to taste)
1   teaspoon black pepper (or to taste)
1   tablespoon salt (or to taste)

Remove skin and fat from chicken and wash well. Bring 2 quarts of water to a boil. Add chicken. Cover and simmer for a 1/2 hour or until chicken is tender. Remove from water and strip meat from bones. Set meat aside.

Cut fern into 6 inch pieces. Boil with whole onion for a 1/2 hour in 8 cups chicken stock (approximately). Cut green onions in fourths. Add to stock with cayenne pepper, black pepper and chopped garlic. Boil 10 minutes. Add chicken. Boil an additional 10 minutes. Serve with short-grain rice.

CHICKEN SOUP (TRADITIONAL KOREAN STYLE)

1   3 pound whole chicken
6   quarts water
10   dried chestnuts
10   dried red dates
6   peeled garlic pieces
1   cup sweet rice (uncooked)
2   4 inch pieces ginseng

Soak chestnuts and dates for one hour. Soak rice for 30 minutes. Clean the stomach of the chicken. Stuff chicken with chestnuts, dates and ginseng. Put the rice in the chicken last. Sew up chicken and boil on high heat in 6 quarts of water for 2 hours. Ready to Serve.

BEEF RIB SOUP (KALBI)

2   pounds beef ribs
2 1/2   quarts water
1   medium daikon radish
1   round yellow onion
5   cloves garlic
1   teaspoon salt
1/2   teaspoon black pepper

Cut beef ribs in half and boil in a 1/2 quart of water for ten minutes. Drain water and rinse ribs. Boil ribs, peeled whole onion, whole radish, and whole garlic cloves in two quarts of water for a 1/2 hour. Remove radish, set aside and continue boiling ribs, garlic and onion for 30 minutes. Cut whole radish into 2 inch squares and put 1/2 cup per bowl per person and pour soup over top. Store radish separately.

KIM'S MEATBALL SOUP

1   pound ground sirloin
5   green onions, chopped
1/2   yellow onion, chopped
2   tablespoon sesame seeds (roasted)
1   teaspoon chopped garlic
1   tablespoon sesame oil
1/2   teaspoon black pepper
1   tablespoon hot pepper powder
1/2   teaspoon salt
2   eggs

Heat 2 tablespoons sesame oil in a large pan. Mix all ingredients in a bowl. Make walnut-size balls and drop into pan. Fry over low heat, to golden brown. Leave in pan.

Gravy:

2   cups water
3   beef bouillon cubes
6   green onions
1/2   teaspoon sugar
1   tablespoon hot paste

Heat 2 cups water. Add bouillon cubes and dissolve. Add remaining ingredients. Boil well for 10 minutes. When done pour over meatballs and boil for 5 more minutes. Serve with rice.

BEEF SOUP (SOLGULGE GUEK)

1 pound beef (sirloin)
1 pound soybean sprouts
1/3 cup hot red pepper powder
5 green onions, 1-inch long
1 yellow onion
1 tablespoon chopped garlic
1 tablespoon salt
3 jalapeno peppers, chopped
1/2 teaspoon black pepper
2 quarts water
1/4 cup sesame oil

Wash beef and slice in thin strips. On low heat, saute meat for 10 minutes in 1/4 cup sesame oil. Add water and boil for 1/2 hour.

Cut green onions and chop yellow onion and peppers. Wash bean sprouts. Add all ingredients and seasonings to pan. Cook for 10 minutes. Serve with rice.

BEAN SPROUT SOUP WITH BEEF

1 pound beef (sirloin)
1 pound soybean bean sprouts
1 teaspoon chopped garlic
5 green onions, 1-inch long
1 teaspoon hot pepper powder
1 tablespoon soy sauce
8 cups water
1 tablespoon sesame oil

Cut beef into bite-size pieces. Saute in sesame oil for 5 minutes. Add remaining ingredients. Cook for another 10 minutes. Add salt to taste. Serve with rice.

BEEF FOO YUNG SOUP

8 cups water
6 beef bouillon cubes
1/4 teaspoon black pepper
1/2 teaspoon salt (optional)
3 cups rice flour
2 bundles spinach
3 bundles green onions
1 teaspoon chopped garlic
1 tablespoon roasted sesame seeds (optional)
1 tablespoon hot pepper powder
1 leek

Clean green onions and cut into two long halves. Clean spinach and cut into two. Clean and cut leek into 2 long halves. Mix 3 cups water with 3 cups rice flour and set aside.

Place 6 cups of water in a deep pan and add bouillon cubes and bring to a boil. Add all vegetables and ingredients and cook for 5 minutes. Slowly stir in the mixture of 3 cups of water and rice flour and cook for 5 more minutes. May be cooked more if desired. Serves 3-5 people.

Best if served with steamed short grain rice.

HOT FLAVORED SOUP (KIMCHEE GUEK-SUE)

1 cup Kimchee (see recipe for Kimchee)
1 tablespoon sesame seeds (roasted)
1 teaspoon sesame oil
1 quart water
2 tablespoons anchovy soup stock
2 small handfuls (7-14 oz.) Korean noodles (wheat)

Finely chop Kim Chee. Mix with sesame seeds and oil. Set aside.

Bring water to full boil in medium pot. Add soup stock and boil uncovered for 10 minutes. Set aside.

In 2 quarts rapidly boiling water, cook noodles for 10 minutes, or until done. Drain and rinse.

To serve, put noodles in individual serving bowls. Pour anchovy soup over noodles and stir in Kim Chee. Serves 2-3 People.

MUSHROOM BEEF BROTH SOUP

5 cups beef stock
5 cups water
1/2 pound fresh mushrooms, sliced
1 cup leek, 1-inch long
3 asparagus, 1-inch long
1/2 teaspoon chopped garlic
1 tablespoon salt
1/2 teaspoon black pepper
1/2 yellow onion

Boil beef broth well. Cut yellow onion in quarters. Cut leek, mushrooms and asparagus. Add all ingredients to beef broth. Cook for 10 minutes. Add salt to taste. Serve.

TRIPE SOUP

2 beef honeycomb tripe
2 quarts water
1/3 cup hot red pepper powder
1 tablespoon chopped garlic
5 green onions, 1-inch long
3 green jalapeno peppers
1 yellow onion
1/3 cup salt
1 teaspoon black pepper
1/3 cup sesame oil

Slice tripe 2 inches long and 1/2 inch thick. Cut and wash. On low temperature, saute tripe in sesame oil for 10 minutes. Put tripe into 2 quarts and boil for 1/2 hour.

While cooking, wash all vegetables. Cut green onions into 1-inch long pieces. Quarter yellow onion, and then chop. Quarter green jalapeno peppers and remove seeds. Mix all the vegetables in a bowl. Put vegetables and the remaining ingredients into soup. Cook for 10 minutes.

Ready to serve. Best with short grain rice. Serves 5-6 people.

OX TAIL SOUP (KOMTUNG)

3 cloves garlic, whole
1 yellow onion, whole
1 tablespoon salt
3 quarts water
2 pounds ox tail

Bring 5 cups water to a boil. Add ox tails, boil for 5 minutes. Drain and rinse well. Return ox tails to pot, add three quarts water, return to boil. Peel onion and garlic cloves. Place onion, garlic and salt in boiling soup. Cook over medium heat for 1 1/2 hours. Ready to Serve.

CLAM AND BEAN SPROUT SOUP WITH RICE

1 cup rice
1 pound soybean bean sprouts
10 ounces baby clams (precooked)
1 teaspoon chopped garlic
1 teaspoon hot pepper powder
2 green onions, 1-inch long
1 tablespoon soy sauce
12 cups water

Wash rice. Let soak 1/2 hour.

Cook clams in 12 cups water for 20 minutes.

Add rice, and cook for another 10 minutes.

Add remaining ingredients, and cook for 10 more minutes. Add salt to taste. Serves 3-5 people.

SALMON HEAD SOUP

1 salmon head (large)
6 cups water
1 yellow onion
3 green jalapeno peppers, without seeds, quartered
5 garlic cloves, whole
1 tablespoon salt

Optional:

2 green onions

Combine all ingredients in sauce pan and cook for approximately 1/2 hour. Add salt to taste. Serve.

POLLACK SOUP

2 ounces shredded pollack fish (dried)
2 tablespoons sesame oil
3 quarts water
5 green onions, with tops
2 cloves garlic, or 1 teaspoon garlic powder
1 tablespoon hot red pepper powder
2 teaspoons salt, or to taste
2 eggs

Rinse pollack, squeezing out as much water as possible. Saute fish in sesame oil in a large pot for 5 minutes. Add water; boil for 30 minutes.

While soup is boiling, cut onions in 1/2 inch pieces; chop garlic. Add all ingredients to soup except eggs, continuing to boil for 5 minutes. Slowly stir in beaten eggs and cook an additional 5 minutes. Serves 5-6 People. Serve with rice.

CLAM AND BEAN SPROUT SOUP

1 pound soybean bean sprouts
10 ounces baby clams (precooked)
1 teaspoon chopped garlic
1 teaspoon hot pepper powder
2 green onions, 1-inch long
1 tablespoon soy sauce
8 cups water

Put 8 cups water in a pot. Add clams and boil for 10 minutes.

Add remaining ingredients. Cook for another 15 minutes.

Serve with rice.

MUSSEL SEAWEED SOUP

  5   cups water
  2 1/2 ounces seaweed
  2   pounds mussels
  1   teaspoon garlic powder
  1/2   teaspoon salt
  1   tablespoon sesame oil
  1   teaspoon garlic powder

Wash seaweed and soak well. Set aside. Boil 5 cups water. Add mussels and cook for 5 minutes. Remove mussels from shells. Set aside.

Add 3 more cups water to the original 5 cups water. Set aside. Put sesame oil in large sauce pan and saute seaweed for 5 minutes. Add 8 cups water and garlic powder. Boil for 20 minutes. Add mussels and salt. Add salt to taste. Serves 3-4 people.

SHRIMP SEAWEED SOUP

  1   pound shrimp
  8   cups water
  1   teaspoon garlic, chopped
  1   teaspoon salt, or to taste
  2 1/2 ounces seaweed

Wash seaweed and soak well. Set aside. Peel and clean shrimp. Set aside. Boil 8 cups water. Add garlic, salt and seaweed. Boil for approximately 1/2 hour.

Add shrimp and cook for 5 more minutes. Serve.

CRAB SEAWEED SOUP

  1   pound fresh imitation crab meat
  8   cups water
  1   teaspoon garlic, chopped
  1   teaspoon salt, or to taste
  2 1/2 ounces seaweed

Wash seaweed and soak well. Set aside. Boil 8 cups water. Add garlic, salt and seaweed. Boil for approximately 1/2 hour.

Add crab and cook for 5 more minutes. Serve.

SEAWEED DUMPLING SOUP

2 cups rice powder
1/4 teaspoon salt
1 cup water
2 cups sweet rice powder
1/4 cup sesame oil
1 ounce dried seaweed
1 tablespoon garlic salt
3 quarts water
2 pound roast beef

Mix 2 cups rice powder, 1/4 teaspoon salt, and 1 cup water. Mix well, and knead for 10 minutes. Set aside.

Soak seaweed for 1/2 hour, in cold water. Wash well.

Wash beef and cut in very thin slices, about 1-inch long. Mix seaweed, beef and sesame oil, then saute for 10 minutes.

Add 3 quarts water and boil for 1 hour. Add 1 tablespoon of garlic, and boil mixture an additional hour. Make walnut size balls out of dough, and drop into soup.

Cook for 10 minutes. When rice balls rise to the top, they are cooked. Ready to serve. Add salt to taste. Serves 5-6 people.

MUNG BEANS AND RICE SOUP

1 cup short grain rice
2 cups whole mung beans
6 quarts water, divided
1 tablespoon salt, or to taste

Wash rice well; soak in water for a 1/2 hour. Drain and set rice aside.

Wash and rinse beans. Put in heavy pot; cover, and boil rapidly in 5 quarts of water for 1/2 hour, checking to be sure beans don't boil over. Remove cover, and continue to boil rapidly for 1/2 hour. Cool beans. Sieve to separate beans from liquid. Return liquid to cooking pot, and place beans in large bowl.

To loosen and remove bean skins, crush with potato masher or squeeze with hands. Add 1 quart of water, stir, and sieve into separate bowl. Process beans 2 more times, each time stirring in same water used in first processing. Discard bean skins; add liquid to soup in cooking pot. Mix well.

Stirring constantly, boil soup rapidly for 10 minutes. Add rice. Stirring constantly, continue rapid boiling for 20 minutes. Turn temperature to low. Continuing to stir while cooking, simmer for 10 minutes. Add salt. Serves 5-6 people.

RED BEAN SOUP WITH DUMPLINGS

16 ounces Azuki red beans
3 quarts water, divided
2 cups short grain rice
16 ounces sweet rice flour
1/8 teaspoon salt
1 cup warm water

Wash beans well. Boil in 2 quarts of water for a 1/2 hour. Turn heat to low. Simmer for 1 and 1/2 hours, or until done. Drain beans, setting water aside. Mash beans by hand or with blender, food processor, or mixer. Put in large bowl. Add water in which beans were cooked and an additional quart of cold water. Stir beans and water well. Remove bean skins by straining mixture in fine-meshed strainer. Return bean broth to pot. Simmer for 1/2 hour.

While beans are cooking, wash rice well and submerge in water for at least 1/2 hour. Drain and rinse. Set aside.

Also while beans are cooking, prepare rice dumplings: Mix rice flour and salt in bowl. Gradually blend in one cup water. Knead dough for about 20 minutes. Form 1 inch balls. Drop balls into 2 quarts boiling water. Dumplings will rise to surface when cooked, in about 5 minutes. Remove dumplings from water. Set aside.

Add rice to bean broth. Stirring frequently, simmer until rice is done, about 1/2 hour. Add dumplings to soup. Serves 7-8 people.

BEAN SPROUT SOUP (SOY BEANS)

1 pound fresh soybean sprouts (soybean sprouts are white in color with no dark spots)
1 package firm tofu (cut into cubes)
1/2 cup beef stock mix
2 teaspoons sesame seeds (roasted)
1 teaspoon garlic powder
1 green onion (with top)
2 teaspoons hot red bean paste
1 gallon water

Mince onions. Bring water to a boil in a large pot. Add sprouts and all ingredients to the boiling water. Cover and boil for 10 minutes. Ready to Serve.

SOYBEAN SPROUT SOUP WITH BEEF

6 cups water
1 pint soybean sprouts
1 package firm tofu (cut into cubes)
1 tablespoon hot pepper powder
5 green onions, 1 inch long
1 teaspoon garlic, or garlic powder
1 teaspoon salt
1 teaspoon sesame seeds, crushed (roasted)
1/2 pound roast beef
1 teaspoon sesame oil

Wash bean sprouts, and set aside. Cut meat into bite-size pieces, and sauté in sesame oil. Add 6 cups water, and cook to a boil for 20 minutes.

Add soybean sprouts, bean cake, onions, garlic, hot pepper powder, salt and sesame seeds. Mix together, boil for 10 minutes.

Serve with rice. Add salt to taste. Serves 5 people.

HOT FLAVORED SOUP (MUNDU)
WITH RICE CAKES AND POT STICKERS

1-2 **pounds beef neck bones**
1-2 **pounds top round steak, cut in thin slices**
3 **green onions, with tops**
5 **fresh garlic cloves**
1 **tablespoon sesame seeds (roasted)**
1 **tablespoon red pepper powder**
1 **tablespoon soy sauce**
1 **tablespoon sesame oil**
2 **pounds sliced rice cakes**
15 **pot stickers**

Submerge neck bones in water and boil for 10 minutes. Rinse and wash off all blood. Boil bones with round steak for 1 and 1/2 hours or until tender. Remove meat and set beef stock aside.

With fingers, strip meat off bones and tear round steak into small pieces. Place meat in bowl and discard bones. Finely chop green onions and garlic. Add to meat sesame seeds, pepper, soy sauce, and sesame oil. Mix well.

Add meat and spice mixture to meat stock. Boil for 10 minutes. Add rice cakes and pot stickers. Continue boiling for 20 minutes. Remove from heat and set aside for 5 minutes before serving.

Serves 7-8 people.

SOYBEANS & RICE SOUP

1 **cup short grain rice**
2 **cups dry soybeans**
6 **quarts water, divided**
1 **tablespoon salt**

Soak rice for a 1/2 hour in water; drain and set aside. Soak soybeans in water at least 6 hours; drain.

Put 1/2 beans and 1 quart of fresh water into a blender. Process at high speed until beans are finely ground, for approximately 10 minutes. Drain liquid into a large, heavy pot. Repeat with remaining beans. Put processed beans in strainer over pot. Gradually pour 4 remaining quarts of water over beans, mixing and stirring well to remove as much pulp as possible. Discard skins.

Boil liquid under high temperature, stirring constantly, for 20 minutes. Add rice. Continue to boil and stir at high temperature for 10 minutes. Turn heat to low. Boil gently and stir until rice is done, about 1/2 hour. Turn off heat and let stand for 10 minutes. Serves 5-6 people.

SESAME SEED AND RICE SOUP

1   cup rice
2   cups sesame seeds (roasted)
9   cups water
1   teaspoon salt

Combine 2 cups sesame seeds and 5 cups water. Pour into blender. Process approximately 2 minutes. Strain mixture, saving water in a bowl. Repeat entire process until fine particles form. Discard sesame seeds and place liquid in a heavy pot.

Wash and soak rice for 1/2 hour.

Process rice until finely ground. Add rice to liquid and cook over low to medium heat 15 minutes, stirring constantly. Increase to a boil for 5 minutes. Remove from heat and serve.

SWISS CHARD SOUP

1   pound beef cubed steaks, chopped
2   quarts water
1   bundle Swiss chard
1   tablespoon sesame seeds (roasted)
1   teaspoon garlic, chopped
3   green onions, 1-inch long
3   jalapeno peppers, chopped
1/4 teaspoon black pepper
1   tablespoon hot paste
1   tablespoon hot pepper powder
1   teaspoon sesame oil
1   tablespoon soy sauce
1   tablespoon sesame oil

Saute the chopped meat in 1 tablespoon sesame oil for 5 minutes. Add 2 quarts water, and boil for 1/2 hour. Then add remaining ingredients. Cook for 10 minutes. Serve with rice.

TRADITIONAL KOREAN PUMPKIN SOUP

History: This recipe was created by the Kim family for mothers with newborn babies. Picked pumpkins stored in a dry place can be saved for up to five years.

1   medium pumpkin
1   cup dried Korean red beans
7   ounces dried red dates
6   ounces dried chestnuts
2   ounces cinnamon sticks
2   pounds ginger
11 cups water (divided)

Wash and soak dates, chestnuts and beans for one hour. Peel skin off ginger and wash well. Slice into small pieces. Cut 2 inches off the top of the pumpkin. Remove all seeds and wash well. Put all ingredients inside the pumpkin. Then add 5 cups of water. Cook whole pumpkin in a large pan with 6 cups of water for three hours on low heat. Remove cinnamon sticks and ginger. Scoop out soup and serve. You can also eat the inside of the pumpkin.

PUMPKIN SOUP

3   cups water
3   cups pumpkin
1/2 cup dry red beans
1/2 cup sugar
1/2 cup rice flour
1/2 cup sweet rice flour
1/2 teaspoon salt
1   cup water

Cook beans in 5 cups water for approximately 1/2 hour, or unit done well. Set aside. Peel and cube a medium pumpkin. Cook pumpkin in 12 cups water, to a boil. Cook well. Set aside.

Set aside 3 cups of pumpkin. Mix rice and sweet rice flour, with 1/2 teaspoon salt in a large bowl. Add 1 cup water. Do not smash flour lumps. Set aside.

Boil 3 cups water and 3 cups pumpkin for approximately 10 minutes. Add 1/2 cup sugar and 1/2 cup red beans. Gradually add flour mixture. Boil for another 10 minutes, stirring slowly and continuously. Serve.

* Extra pumpkin can be frozen for later use.

RICE SOUP WITH VEGETABLES (YACHE CHOOK)

3   cups cooked rice
3 1/2   cups water
1   cup spinach (chopped)
2   green onions (chopped)
1/4   teaspoon garlic salt
1/4   teaspoons salt (optional)
3   cubes chicken flavored bouillon

Optional:
1   egg, yolk only

Bring 3 1/2 cups of water to a boil and add bouillon cubes. Add rice and cook for about 4 to 5 minutes on low heat. Add spinach, onions, garlic powder, and salt. Ready to serve. Add well beaten egg yolk before serving. Serves 2-3 people.

COLD CUCUMBER SOUP (NENGKUK)

1   large (English) cucumber
3   cups water
1   tablespoon vinegar
1   tablespoon sesame seeds (roasted)
1   teaspoon garlic powder
1   teaspoon sugar
1   hot red pepper (optional)

Wash cucumber. Slice diagonally into 1/8 inch pieces. Cut pieces lengthwise into 1/8 inch strips. Put in small bowl. Stir in all other ingredients except pepper.

If you wish to add a pepper, remove seeds first and slice into very thin strips. Serve chilled.

VEGETARIAN EGGDROP SOUP

1/2   yellow onion, chopped
3   green onions, chopped
3   eggs, beaten
3   cups water
1   package firm tofu, cubed
1/2   teaspoon garlic powder
1/2   teaspoon salt, or to taste.
1/4   teaspoon black pepper

Boil 3 cups water. Add green and yellow onions, cook for 5 minutes. Add bean cake and seasonings. Cook for 5 more minutes.

Beat eggs together and slowly pour into soup. Don't mix. When eggs are firm, stir. Serve with rice.

Stews (CHIGHE)

CHICKEN WING DRUMSTICK STEW

6   cups water
20 chicken wing drumsticks
2   medium potatoes, cubed
5   carrots, cubed
1   yellow onion, quartered
3   cups leek
1/2 teaspoon chopped garlic
1   tablespoon hot pepper powder
1/2 teaspoon hot paste
2   jalapeno peppers, without seeds, quartered
3   green onions, 1-inch long pieces
1/4 teaspoon black pepper
1/2 teaspoon salt, or to taste
2   cups asparagus, 1-inch long pieces

Cook drumsticks in 5 cups water for 5 minutes. Rinse drumsticks. Boil 6 more cups water with chicken wing drumsticks for approximately 1/2 hour.

Cut carrots and potatoes and add to chicken. Cook for 10 minutes.

Quarter yellow onion. Cut bottoms off of green onions and wash. Then cut into 1-inch long pieces. Quarter jalapeno peppers. Cut leek into 1-inch long pieces too. Then quarter each round. Cut asparagus into 1-inch long sections.

Add all ingredients to pan and cook for another 5 minutes. Serve.

HOT CURRY STEW WITH CHICKEN

5   chicken thighs
1   leek
1   yellow onion, cubed
5   medium carrots, 1-inch long sections
5   small potatoes, quartered
1   tablespoon salt (approximately)
2   ounces curry sauce mix, or to taste
1/2 cup cornstarch
1   cup water
1   teaspoon garlic powder

Optional:
1/4 teaspoon black pepper

Cook chicken in 8 cups water for approximately 5 minutes to remove blood, then rinse. Throw away water. Boil chicken again in 6 1/2 cups more water for approximately 20 minutes.

Cut stalk of leek into 1-inch long sections. Don't use the leaves. Cut each stalk round into fourths. Cut onion in half and largely cube to about the size of the meat. Peel carrots and cut off ends. Cut into 1-inch long rounds. Peel potatoes and quarter.

When meat is done, add potatoes and carrots and cook for 10 minutes. Add leek and yellow onions and cook for another 5 minutes. Mix cornstarch and water in a bowl. Slowly add to stew. Add black pepper, salt, garlic powder, salt, and curry sauce mix. Serve with rice. Serves 5 people.

SPICY CHICKEN STEW (CHIGHE)

(See color photograph.)

5   chicken thighs
2   medium potatoes
3   medium carrots
1   medium yellow onion
6   green onions, with tops
1   tablespoon red bean paste,
     or 1 tablespoon curry powder
1/2 teaspoon garlic salt
1/4 teaspoon black pepper
1   teaspoon granulated sugar

Remove skin and fat from chicken thighs. Cut each thigh into three parts. Peel potatoes and carrots and cut into pieces about 2 inches long by 1 inch wide. Peel yellow onion. Cut it in half; then continue to halve pieces to make 8 parts. Cut green onions in fourths.

Boil 8 cups of water. Add chicken and cook for 20 minutes. Check to be sure chicken is cooked by poking it with a fork. If the fork goes in smoothly, the chicken is done.

Add remaining ingredients, and continue boiling for another 20 minutes. Serves 5-6 people. Serve in bowls with short-grain rice as a side dish.

CHICKEN STEW WITH SOYBEAN CAKE

3   cups water
1/2 chicken
1/2 yellow onion, quartered
3   jalapeno peppers
3   green onions
1   teaspoon garlic, chopped
1   teaspoon hot pepper powder
1/2 teaspoon salt, or to taste
6   cups water
14   ounces soybean cake, cubed

Cut chicken into cubes. Boil in 3 cups water for 5 minutes. Drain and wash well. Add 6 cups water to chicken and boil for 20 more minutes.

Add all vegetables and cook for 10 minutes. Check tenderness. Serve with rice.

CHICKEN WING STEW

5   cups chicken wings, cut in three
1   cup soy sauce
1/4 cup sugar
2   cups water
1   teaspoon black pepper
1   tablespoon sesame oil
1   tablespoon sesame seeds (roasted)
1   tablespoon chopped garlic
3   medium potatoes, cubed
5   carrots, cubed

Cut chicken, potatoes and carrots. Mix all ingredients in a pot. Cook for 1/2 hour. Add salt to taste. Serve.

CHIGHE
(Spicy Chicken Stew)

KIM'S GINGER-CHICKEN STEW

5   chicken thighs
1   yellow onion, quartered
1   cup soy sauce
1/2 cup white vinegar
1   cup water
1/2 teaspoon ginger, chopped

Optional:
1   teaspoon sugar

Mix soy sauce, vinegar and water. Put in a sauce pan. Peel skins off chicken and wash. Put in sauce pan. Cook for 10 minutes. Add ginger and onion. Slowly cook for another 15 minutes. Check to see when done. Serve. Serves 1-2 people.

KIM'S CHICKEN STEW

5   chicken thighs
1   yellow onion, quartered
3   pieces of garlic, whole
3   green onions, 1-inch long
1   cup soy sauce
1/2 cup white vinegar
1   cup water

Optional:
1   teaspoon sugar

Mix soy sauce, vinegar and water. Put in a sauce pan. Peel skins off chicken and wash. Put in sauce pan also. Cook for 10 minutes. Add onions and garlic. Slowly cook for another 15 minutes. Serve. Serves 1-2 people.

HOT CHICKEN STEW WITH CARROTS

5   cups water
8   cups water
1   chicken, bite-size pieces
3   jalapeno peppers, without seeds, quartered
5   green onions, 1-inch long pieces
1   yellow onion
1   tablespoon chopped garlic
1   tablespoon red pepper powder, or to taste
1   tablespoon sesame seeds (roasted)
1/2 teaspoon black pepper
5   carrots, cubed
5   medium potatoes, cubed
1/3 cup soy sauce

Heat 5 cups water. Remove bone from chicken and chop. Cook chicken in 5 cups water for 5 minutes and then rinse. Boil 8 cups water and add chicken. Cook on high for 10 minutes. Turn heat low and cook for 45 minutes.

Add 2 cups water to pan. Quarter yellow onion and then slice through the middle. Cut remaining vegetables. Add all ingredients to soup. Cook for 10 minutes. Add salt to taste. Serve.

HOT SPICY CHICKEN THIGH STEW (CHIGHE)

6 chicken thighs
1 yellow onion
5 jalapeno peppers
4 green onions, with tops
5 garlic cloves
2 tablespoons hot red bean paste
1 teaspoon sugar
1/4 teaspoon black pepper
5 cups water

Remove skin and fat from chicken thighs. Peel onion; slice into 8 pieces. Cut peppers in half lengthwise and remove seeds. Cut green onions into fourths. Finely chop garlic. Set aside.

Boil 5 cups of water. Add chicken and cook for 20 minutes. Check to be sure chicken is cooked by inserting fork; fork should go in smoothly.

Add remaining ingredients, and continue boiling for another 20 minutes. Serve.

TURKEY STEW

2 green onions, 1-inch long
3 medium carrots, 1-inch long
2 medium potatoes, quartered
1/2 yellow onion, quartered
2 tablespoons hot paste
1 pound turkey, cubed
5 cups water
1/2 teaspoon chopped garlic

Boil cubed turkey in 5 cups water, with garlic and hot paste for 20 minutes. Add potatoes, carrots and onions. Boil for 10 more minutes. Serve with rice.

STEW (THOK BOK KAY)

1 package (1 quart) Korean rice cakes (Thok), about 3" long by 1/2" diameter pieces
1 pound sirloin steak
5 fish cakes (tempura)
1 tablespoon sesame oil
3 cups water
1 medium yellow onion
5 green onions, with tops
1 tablespoon hot red bean paste
1 teaspoon sugar (optional)
1 teaspoon black pepper (optional)
1 tablespoon red pepper powder
1 teaspoon garlic powder
1 tablespoon sesame seeds (roasted)

First boil rice cakes in 1 quart water (preheat) for 5 minutes. Then rinse in cold water and set aside, drained of the water.

Prepare onions: Peel, quarter and slice onions into 3/4 inch pieces. Cut the green onions into 2 inch pieces. Set aside onions.

Slice meat into thin slices. Put sesame oil in large pan, add meat and the garlic powder. Saute on low temperature for 5 minutes, stirring occasionally.

Add 3 cups of water, hot bean paste and red pepper to the pan, and boil 5 minutes. Add previously prepared rice cakes, onions, sesame seeds and fish cake. Optional: Add black pepper. Stir occasionally. Boil another 5 minutes. Optional: Add 1 teaspoon sugar. Serves 5-6 People.

HOT BEEF ASPARAGUS STEW

1/2	pound beef (sirloin), bite-size pieces
6	asparagus, 1-inch long
1	yellow onion
1/2	pound mushrooms, sliced
1	tablespoon sesame oil
2	cups water
1	tablespoon hot pepper powder
1/4	teaspoon black pepper
1	teaspoon chopped garlic
1	tablespoon sesame seeds (roasted)
1/4	teaspoon salt
1	green jalapeno pepper, without seeds, quartered
3	green onions, 1-inch long

Put sesame oil in a small sauce pan. Saute beef for 5 minutes. Add 2 cups water. Boil for 20 minutes.

Quarter yellow onion and then cut through the middle. Cut jalapeno peppers, green onions, mushrooms and asparagus. Add hot pepper powder and stir. Add remaining ingredients and boil for 5 minutes. Ready to serve. Serves 2 people.

KIM'S HOT BEEF STEW

1	pound roast beef, bite-size pieces
8	medium potatoes
5	carrots
3	pieces celery
1	yellow onion
11	cups water
1	cup hot paste
2	tablespoons hot pepper powder
1	tablespoon chopped garlic
1	tablespoon soy sauce
1	teaspoon salt
1	tablespoon black pepper
2	tablespoons sesame seeds (roasted)
5	green onions, 1-inch long

Boil water, hot paste, hot pepper powder, garlic, soy sauce, salt, black pepper, sesame seeds and sugar together for 10 minutes. Add meat and cook for 20 more minutes. Cube potatoes. Cut carrots 1 1/2 inches long. Cut celery 2 inches long. Quarter yellow onion. Put carrots and potatoes in soup and boil for 10 minutes. Then add celery and onions. Cook for 10 minutes. Serve with rice.

HOT CURRY STEW WITH BEEF

2   pounds boneless stew beef
1   leek
1   yellow onion, cubed
5   medium carrots, 1-inch long sections
5   small potatoes, quartered
1   tablespoon salt (approximately)
1/2   cup cornstarch
1   cup water
1   teaspoon garlic powder
2   ounces curry sauce mix, or to taste

Optional:
1/4   teaspoon black pepper

Largely cube beef. Boil in 6 cups water for 10 minutes. Take meat out and rinse. Throw away water. Boil again in 12 more cups water for approximately 45 minutes. Check meat.

Cut stalk of leek into 1-inch long sections. Don't use the leaves. Cut each stalk round into fourths. Cut onion in half and largely cube each half to about the size of the meat. Peel carrots and cut off ends. Cut into 1-inch long rounds. Peel potatoes and quarter.

When meat is done add potatoes and carrots and cook for 10 minutes. Add leek and yellow onions and cook for another 5 minutes. Mix cornstarch and water in a bowl. Add cornstarch mixture, black pepper, salt and curry sauce mix. Serve with rice. Serves 5 people.

HOT BEEF AND POTATO STEW

3   medium potatoes
3   ounces oriental style starch noodles
1   pound beef (sirloin)
1   yellow onion, sliced
5   green onions, 1-inch long
6   jalapeno peppers
2   tablespoons soybean paste
1   teaspoon red pepper powder
1/2   teaspoon sugar
3   cups water
1   teaspoon salt

Peel and wash potatoes. Cut into cubes. Boil noodles for 10 minutes. Rinse with cold water and drain.

Cut beef into bite-size pieces. Saute with 1 tablespoon soy sauce. Add 3 cups water, all seasonings, and soybean paste. Stir and boil for 10 minutes.

Add the potatoes. Cook for 10 minutes. Then add noodles, onions and peppers. Add salt to taste. Serve with rice. Serves 3-5 people.

HOT PORK AND POTATO STEW

3 ounces oriental style starch noodles
1 pound pork
3 medium potatoes
1 yellow onion, sliced
5 green onions, 1-inch long
5 jalapeno peppers
2 tablespoons hot bean paste
1 teaspoon red pepper powder
1 tablespoon garlic
14 ounces bean cake, bite-size pieces
1/4 teaspoon black pepper
1/2 teaspoon sugar
3 cups water
1 teaspoon salt

Peel and wash potatoes. Cut into cubes. Rinse with cold water and drain.

Cut pork into bite-size pieces. Saute with 1 tablespoon soy sauce. Add 3 cups water, all the seasonings and hot bean paste. Stir. Boil for 10 minutes.

Add the potatoes and cook for 10 minutes. Then add the noodles, onions, peppers, and bean cake. Cook for 5 more minutes. Add salt to taste. Serve with rice. Serves 3-5 people.

HOT-SPICY BEEF STEW (CHIGHE)

1/2 pound beef roast
1 quart water
1 tablespoon hot red bean paste
1 teaspoon garlic powder
14 ounces regular firm tofu
5 green onions
1 teaspoon salt
2-3 jalapeno peppers, if desired

Cut meat into thin slices. Boil for 5 minutes in water to cover; rinse to remove blood. Return meat to washed pan. Add 1 quart of water, hot bean paste, and garlic powder. Boil for 10 minutes.

Cut tofu into 1 inch cubes, quarter and deseed green pepper, cut onions into 1 inch pieces. Quarter and deseed jalapeno peppers. Add tofu, onions, salt and jalapeno peppers to meat mixture. Boil an additional 10 minutes. Serves 3-5 people.

BEEF HONEYCOMB TRIPE STEW

2 pounds beef honeycomb tripe, bite-size pieces
1 large yellow onion, cubed
5 cups leek, 1-inch long pieces
5 jalapeno peppers, without seeds, quartered
2 tablespoons hot pepper powder, or to taste
1 teaspoon salt or to taste
1/2 teaspoon black pepper
1/2 teaspoon garlic, chopped

Boil tripe in 8 cups water, for approximately 1/2 hour. Check texture of tripe. If rubbery, cook until the tripe texture is very soft. Cut yellow onion and jalapeno peppers. Cut bottoms off of green onions and wash. Then cut into 1-inch long pieces. Cut leek and then wash. Add all ingredients to pan. Cook for 5 minutes and serve.

HOT CURRY DEER STEW

2   pounds deer meat
1   leek
1   yellow onion, cubed
5   medium carrots, 1-inch long sections
5   small potatoes quartered
1   tablespoon salt (approximately)
1/2 cup cornstarch
1   cup water
1   teaspoon garlic powder

Optional:
1/4 teaspoon black pepper

Largely cube deer meat. Boil in 6 cups water for 10 minutes. Take meat out and rinse. Throw away water. Boil again in 12 more cups water for approximately 45 minutes. Check meat.

Cut stalk of leek into 1-inch long sections. Don't use the leaves. Cut each stalk round into fourths. Cut onion in half and largely cube each half to about the size of the meat. Peel carrots and cut off ends. Cut into 1-inch long rounds. Peel potatoes and quarter.

When meat is done add potatoes and carrots and cook for 10 minutes. Add leek and yellow onion and cook for another 5 minutes. Mix cornstarch and water in a bowl. Add slowly to stew. Add black pepper, salt, garlic powder and curry sauce mix. Serve with rice. Serves 5 people.

KOREAN PORK STEW

1   teaspoon sugar
14 ounces soybean cake
1/2 yellow onion
5   green onions, 1-inch long
2   jalapeno peppers
1   teaspoon hot pepper powder
1   teaspoon hot paste
1   teaspoon soybean paste
1   cup water
1   teaspoon chopped garlic
1/2 pound pork
1   teaspoon roasted sesame seeds (roasted)

Boil 1 cup water. Add garlic, hot paste and soybean paste. Slice pork and add. Boil for 20 minutes.

Slice green onions and add. Cut yellow onions in slices and add. Slice soybean cake into 1/2 inch thick slices. Fry to a golden brown. Then cut into squares and add. Ready to serve.

DEER MEAT STEW

1 pound deer meat, largely cubed
2 medium potatoes, cubed
3 carrots, cubed
1 medium yellow onion, cubed
5 cups leek, 1-inch long pieces
1 tablespoon hot pepper powder
1/4 teaspoon black pepper
1/2 teaspoon salt
1/2 teaspoon garlic, chopped
3 jalapeno peppers, without seeds, quartered

Boil deer meat in 3 cups water for 5 minutes. Wash off meat. Boil meat again in 5 more cups clean water for 1/2 hour. Check meat. Add carrots, garlic, hot pepper powder and potatoes. Boil for 10 more minutes. Add onions, leek, jalapeno peppers, black pepper, salt and cook for another 5 minutes. Serves 2-3 people.

HOT DUCK STEW WITH CARROTS

5 cups water
8 cups water
1 duck, bite-size pieces
3 jalapeno peppers, without seeds, quartered
5 green onions, 1-inch long
1 yellow onion
1 tablespoon chopped garlic
1/2 cup hot paste
1 tablespoon sesame seeds (roasted)
1/2 teaspoon black pepper
5 carrots, cubed
5 medium potatoes, cubed
1/3 cup soy sauce

Heat 5 cups water. Chop duck. Cook duck in 5 cups preheated water for 5 minutes. Rinse duck. Boil 8 cups water and add duck. Cook on high for 10 minutes. Turn heat low and cook for another 45 minutes. Add 2 cups water.

Quarter yellow onion and then slice through the middle. Cut remaining vegetables. Add all ingredients to soup. Cook for 10 minutes. Add salt to taste. Serve.

HOT DUCK STEW

5   **cups water**
8   **cups water**
1   **duck, bite-size pieces**
5   **jalapeno peppers, without seeds, quartered**
5   **asparagus, 1-inch long**
2   **cups leek, 2-inch long**
1   **tablespoon chopped garlic**
1   **yellow onion**
1   **tablespoon hot pepper powder**
1   **tablespoon sesame seeds (roasted)**
1/3   **cup soy sauce**
1/2   **teaspoon black pepper**

Heat 6 cups water. Chop duck. Cook duck in 5 cups preheated water for 5 minutes. Rinse duck. Boil 8 cups water and add duck. Cook on high for 10 minutes. Turn heat low and cook for another 45 minutes.

Quarter yellow onion and then slice through middle. Cut remaining vegetables. Add all ingredients to soup. Cook for 10 minutes. Serve.

SHRIMP & CLAM STEW (CHIGHE)

1   **pound baby clams**
3   **tablespoons hot red bean paste**
5   **cups water**
1   **tablespoon chopped fresh garlic**

Rinse clams. Combine clams, red bean paste, water and fresh garlic and boil for 30 minutes.

5   **green onions**
1/2   **medium yellow onion**
14   **ounces tofu, medium**
2   **jalapeno peppers**
1   **pound shrimp, precooked**

Cut green onions into 2 inch pieces. Dice yellow onions. Cut tofu into 1 inch squares. Quarter jalapeno peppers and remove seeds. Add onions, tofu, and boil for ten minutes. Add shrimp to boiling soup. Then remove from heat. Ready to Serve.

SOLE FISH STEW (CHIGHE)

5 trimmed rex sole fish
1 cup soy sauce
1/2 cup hot pepper powder
1 tablespoon garlic powder
2 tablespoons sugar
1 bunch green onions
2 cups water
1 medium daikon radish
1 large yellow round onion
2 jalapeno peppers

Cut radish into 2 inch by 1/4 inch pieces. Clean and cut fish in half. Mix soy sauce, water, pepper, garlic, and sugar in small bowl. Line pan with radish and then put the fish on top of the radish. Then pour the soy sauce mixture over the fish and radish. Cover pan and cook on high heat for 20 minutes.

Cut green onions into 2 inch pieces and quarter the yellow onion. Quarter and remove the seeds of the jalapeno peppers. Reduce heat to low then add green onions, yellow onions, and jalapenos. Cover and simmer for thirty minutes. Serve with rice.

HOT AND SPICY SNAPPER STEW WITH BEEF (CHIGHE)

1 lb. beef roast
4 fillets (medium, about 7") Emperor Snapper or Red Snapper
2 quarts water
1/4 cup soy sauce
1 daikon radish (medium) large Japanese radish
2 tablespoons dry powdered red pepper or flakes
2 tablespoons hot red bean paste
1 medium size round onion
2 bundles green onions
1 tub (14 ounces) regular firm tofu
2 jalapeno peppers (optional)
1 tablespoon salt

Cut beef roast into 1 inch chunks. In a large pan, boil 5 cups water. Add beef chunks and boil for 20 minutes on high heat.

Add water, soy sauce, chopped garlic, hot bean paste, and two deseeded, quartered jalapeno peppers. Then add quartered fish, green onions cut into 2 inch pieces, round onion cut into about 1 inch chunks, tofu (1 inch chunks) and the red pepper. Stir occasionally.

Boil on high for 30 minutes, stirring occasionally. Add salt as desired and serve. Usually served with rice.

HOT SNAPPER STEW (CHIGHE)

4   medium size fillets of Emperor Snapper or Red Snapper
2   quarts water
1/4   cup soy sauce
1   daikon radish (medium size or large Japanese radish)
2   tablespoons dry powdered red pepper or flakes
2   tablespoons hot red bean paste
2   bundles green onions
5   garlic cloves (chopped)
1   medium size round onion
1   tablespoon salt
14   ounce regular firm Tofu
2   jalapeno peppers (optional)

In large pan add water, soy sauce, chopped garlic, hot bean paste, and daikon cut into cubes about one inch size. Add two quartered and deseeded jalapeno peppers. Bring to rapid boil for 10 minutes, then reduce temperature to low and boil for 20 minutes.

Add fish, green onion cut into 2 inch pieces, yellow onion cut into 1 inch pieces, one inch pieces of tofu and red pepper. The fish fillets should be cut at an angle into about 3 good size pieces (approx. 3 inches). Stir occasionally.

Add salt as desired and serve with rice.

RED SNAPPER STEW (CHIGHE)

2   pounds Red Snapper
1/2   yellow onion (chopped)
5   green onions (chopped)
1/2   teaspoon garlic (chopped)
3   jalapeno peppers
1/4   teaspoon salt
3   cups water

Scale and wash fish well. Add 3 cups of water and the Red Snapper to a pan. Quarter the jalapeno peppers and remove the seeds. Add the peppers, onions, garlic and salt. More salt may be added to taste if desired.

Boil on high heat for about 20 minutes. Serves 1-2 people.

KOREAN STYLE SEAFOOD STEW
(HAEMUL CHONGUL)

1/2	pound petrale sole fillet
2	jumbo shrimp
3	clams
3	muscles
3	squid
1	pound beef roast
5	miniature octopuses
8	cups water
1	tablespoon garlic, chopped
1	yellow onion
5	green onions, chopped
2	tablespoons hot paste
1	tablespoon red pepper powder
1	teaspoon black pepper
1	teaspoon salt

Boil water and seasonings and garlic for 10 minutes.

Cut beef into bite-size pieces. Wash and clean clams, shrimp, fillet, muscles, squid and octopuses.

Add all meat, seafood and onions to soup. Cook for 15 minutes. Add salt to taste. Serve with rice.

HOT ROCK COD STEW

2	zucchini
5	green onions, 1-inch long
1/2	yellow onion
1	cup white radish
3	jalapeno peppers
2	tablespoons hot paste
1	tablespoon hot pepper powder
1	teaspoon salt
1	teaspoon soy sauce
1	teaspoon chopped garlic
1	pound rock cod fillet
1/2	pound beef
8	cups water

Optional:
1	tablespoon sugar

Boil 8 cups water. Cut rock cod fillet and beef into bite-size pieces. Cut 1/2 yellow onion into 3 pieces, and white radish into strips 2 inches long and 1-inch thick. Add beef, hot paste, garlic, soy sauce, salt and pepper powder to boiling water. Cook for 20 minutes.

Then add zucchini, onions, radish, peppers and meat. Cook for 15 minutes. Add sugar, if desired. Cook 10 more minutes.

Serve with rice.

TROUT STEW

1   cup water
1   8-inch long trout, cut in thirds
14 ounces bean cake
1   cup soy sauce
1/2 teaspoon chopped garlic
2   teaspoons hot paste
3   green onions, 1-inch long
3   jalapeno peppers, without seeds, quartered
1   yellow onion, quartered
1   teaspoon sugar

Clean and wash trout. Cut bean cake lengthwise and then 1/2 inch wide strips across. Put fish in a sauce pan. Put bean cake on top of fish. Mix soy sauce, garlic, hot pepper powder, hot paste, and sugar in a bowl. Pour over bean cake. Top with green and yellow onions, and peppers. Cook for 1/2 hour. Serve.

HOT AND SPICY HERRING STEW

2   green onions, 1-inch long
1   tablespoon sesame seeds (roasted)
2   tablespoons hot pepper powder
1   cup water
1   tablespoon garlic, chopped
1   tablespoon hot paste
1   teaspoon sugar
1   pound herring
14 ounces soybean bean cake, cubed
1/2 yellow onion, quartered
1/2 teaspoon salt

Clean herring.

Mix all ingredients except fish, in a bowl. Put fish in a sauce pan. Pour half of the sauce over it. Cook for 5 minutes.

Put soybean cake over the fish. Then put green and yellow onions on top of the cake. Cover with remaining sauce. Cook for 10 minutes on low temperature. Ready to serve.

CRAB AND BEANCAKE STEW

2   chicken bouillon cubes
3   cups water
1/4 ounces firm beancake
1/2 pound crab
6   green onions 1-inch long
1/2 yellow onion, cubed
1/2 teaspoon garlic powder
1/2 teaspoon hot pepper powder
1/4 teaspoon black pepper

Boil bouillon cubes with 3 cups water and dissolve. Add garlic powder, hot pepper powder, and black pepper. Stir. Boil for 10 minutes.

Add beancake, crab, green onions, and yellow onion and stir. Serve with rice. Serves 2-3 people.

CLAM AND BEANCAKE STEW

10 ounces baby clams
14 ounces firm beancake, cubed
1   medium potato, cubed
1   medium carrot, cubed
1/2 yellow onion, cubed
6   green onions, 1-inch long slices
1/2 teaspoon salt, or to taste
1/2 teaspoon garlic powder
1/2 pound button mushrooms, sliced
5   asparagus, 1-inch long pieces
1/4 teaspoon black pepper

Strain juice from baby clams can and save. Add water to juice to make 3 cups and set aside clams.

Cube carrot and potato. Add salt, black pepper, garlic powder, carrot and potato to water mixture, and cook for 10 minutes.

Cube beancake and yellow onion. Wash off green onions and cut roots off. Cut into 1-inch long sections. Slice mushrooms and asparagus into 1-inch long pieces. Add green onions, beancake, yellow onion, mushrooms and asparagus to stew and cook for another 5 minutes.

Ready to serve with rice. Serves 2-3 people.

CLAM STEW

5 cups water
1-2 pounds little neck clams
16 ounces firm bean cake, cubed
1/2 pound button mushrooms, sliced
1/2 cup bamboo shoots
10 squid, cut into fourths
1 zucchini
3 cups leek
1 yellow onion, 1-inch long
5 green onions, 1-inch long
3 jalapeno peppers, quartered, without seeds
1/2 teaspoon chopped garlic
1 tablespoon hot pepper powder
1 tablespoon hot paste
1 teaspoon sugar
1/4 teaspoon black pepper
1 medium potato, cubed
1 teaspoon salt

Boil 5 cups water, salt, hot pepper powder, hot paste, and garlic well for 20 minutes. Wash and scrub clams. Cube bean cake. Slice mushrooms. Wash and clean squid and then cut each piece into fourths. Cut zucchini down the middle and then cube. Cut leek into 1-inch thick rounds. Then cut each round into fourths. Quarter yellow onion. Wash green onions and cut bottoms off. Then cut into 1-inch long pieces. Quarter jalapeno peppers and remove seeds. Peel potato and cube.

Add all ingredients to pan. Cook for approximately 10 minutes, or until done. Serves 3-5 people.

CRAB AND SHRIMP STEW

1/2 pound crab meat
1/2 pound shrimp
16 ounces firm bean cake, cubed
1 tablespoon red pepper powder
1 teaspoon salt
1 teaspoon garlic, chopped
6 green onions, 1 inch long
1 medium yellow onion, cubed
2 cups leek
5 cups water

Boil water, hot pepper powder, salt and garlic for approximately 20 minutes. Cube bean cake. Cut bottoms off of green onions and wash. Then cut into 1-inch long pieces. Cut leek into 1-inch long pieces. Take each round and quarter it. Cut yellow onion. Peel and wash shrimp. Add crab, shrimp, leek, green onion, yellow onion, and bean cake to soup. Cook for approximately 5 minutes. Serve.

SALMON HEAD STEW WITH ZUCCHINI

10 6-inch long zucchini
1   pound salmon head
2   green onions, 1-inch long
1   yellow onion, quartered
3   jalapeno peppers, without seeds, quartered
1/2 teaspoon chopped garlic
1   cup soy sauce
1   tablespoon red pepper powder
1/2 teaspoon sugar

Slice zucchini down the middle, and then cut in half. Slice fish head in half. Put in bottom of large pan. Put zucchini on top of fish head. Chop onions. Put peppers and onions on top of zucchini. Mix garlic, soy sauce, red pepper powder and sugar in a bowl. Pour over onions and peppers. Add 1 cup water around edges of pan.

Cook on high temperature for 10 minutes. Cook for approximately 10 more minutes. Serve.

SALMON HEAD STEW WITH RADISH

1   pound salmon head
1   medium radish
2   green onions, 1-inch long
1   yellow onion, quartered
3   jalapeno peppers, without seeds, quartered
1/2 teaspoon chopped garlic
1   cup soy sauce
1   tablespoon red pepper powder
1/2 teaspoon sugar

Peel radish. Cut down the middle and then make 1/2 inch thick slices. Slice the fish head in half. Put radishes in bottom of large pan, and place fish heads over the radish. Chop onions. Put peppers and onions on top of fish head. Mix garlic, soy sauce, red pepper powder and sugar in a small bowl. Pour over onions and peppers. Add 1 cup water around the edges of the pan.

Cook on high temperature for 10 minutes. Turn heat down and cook for another 10 minutes. Ready to Serve.

MISO STEW

2 tablespoons shiro miso soybean paste
2 cups water
3 green onions, 1-inch long
1/2 yellow onion, quartered
14 ounces soft soybean cake, cubed
1/2 teaspoon garlic powder
2 jalapeno peppers, without seeds, quartered
2 asparagus, 1-inch long

Boil 2 cups water. Add garlic powder and bean paste. Boil for approximately 10 minutes.

Add soybean cake, asparagus, jalapeno peppers and onions. Cook for 5 more minutes. Serve.

VEGETARIAN BEANCAKE STEW

1 cup water
1 cup soy sauce
1 tablespoon cooking oil
14 ounces beancake
5 green onions, 1-inch long
1 tablespoon garlic, minced
1 tablespoon sesame seeds, crushed (roasted)
1 tablespoon sesame oil
1 tablespoon hot pepper powder

Combine all ingredients except beancake and cooking oil. Set aside. Cut beancake lengthwise. Cut in 1/2 inch thick slices. Fry beancake in cooking oil until golden brown.

In same pan layer beancake and sauce, with beancake on bottom. Cook covered over low heat for 10 minutes. Serve with rice.

HOT ASPARAGUS VEGETARIAN STEW

6 asparagus, 1-inch long
1 yellow onion
1/2 pound mushrooms sliced
2 cups water
1 tablespoon hot pepper powder
1/4 teaspoon black pepper
1/2 teaspoon chopped garlic
1 tablespoon sesame seeds (roasted)
1/4 teaspoon salt
1 green jalapeno pepper, without seeds, quartered
3 green onions, 1-inch long

Put 2 cups water in a small sauce pan. Add garlic and hot pepper powder. Boil for 20 minutes.

Add remaining ingredients and cook 5 minutes. Serves 2 people.

BEANCAKE STEW

1 tablespoon soybean paste
2 cups water
3 green onions 1-inch long
1/2 yellow onion, quartered
1/4 ounces firm soybean cake, cubed
1/2 teaspoon garlic powder
1 teaspoon sugar
2 asparagus, 1-inch long

Boil 2 cups water. Add garlic powder and bean paste. Boil for approximately 10 minutes.

Add soybean cake, asparagus, sugar and onions. Cook for 5 more minutes. Serve.

HOT BEEF AND BEANCAKE STEW

1   cup soy sauce
1   tablespoon cooking oil
14   ounces beancake
5   green onions, 1-inch long
1   tablespoon garlic, minced
1   tablespoon sesame seeds (roasted), crushed
1   cup water
1   tablespoon sesame oil
1   tablespoon hot pepper powder
1   pound roast beef, cut in strips

Combine all ingredients except cooking oil, beef, sesame oil and beancake in small bowl. Stir well. Heat cooking oil. Cut bean cake length wise, and then cut in 1/2 inch thick slices. Fry bean cake until golden brown. Remove from pan and drain.

Saute roast beef in 1 tablespoon sesame oil for 3-5 minutes. In the same pan layer beef, beancake and sauce in that order. Cook over low temperature for 10 minutes, covered. Serve with rice.

RADISH & PUMPKIN STEW (CHIGHE)

1   quart radish pumpkin Kim Chee
1   quart water

Boil on medium heat for 30 minutes. This chighe is best when it is served with short grain rice.

HOT BEAN PASTE STEW

1/2   pound beef
14   ounces Japanese style soybean cake
1/3   cup hot bean paste
5   green onions
3   jalapeno peppers
1   teaspoon garlic, chopped
4   cups water

Cut beef into thin strips, 1-inch squares. Add water and beef together in a pan. Boil for 10 minutes.

Cut onions into 1-inch pieces. Chop garlic. Quarter peppers and take seeds out. Cut bean cake into 1-inch cubes. Combine vegetables and bean cake in a bowl. Set aside.

Add to beef and water. Boil another 10 minutes. Serve with rice.

BEAN PASTE STEW (CHIGHE)

1/2   yellow onion
5   green onions, with tops
1-2   jalapeno peppers, or to taste
2   cloves garlic or 1/8 teaspoon garlic powder
14   ounces regular firm tofu
1   tablespoon miso (soy bean paste)
1   tablespoon soup stock powder (clam, beef, or anchovy)
6   cups water

Cut yellow onion into thin slices. Cut green onions into 2 inch pieces. Quarter pepper(s) lengthwise and deseed. Mince garlic cloves. Cut tofu into 1 inch cubes.

Blend miso, soup stock powder and water in a pot. Cover and boil rapidly for 5 minutes. Add vegetables and tofu and continue boiling for 10 minutes. Ready to Serve.

Notes

Sauces

HOT SAUCE

16 ounces malt powder
5   pounds sweet rice powder
1   cup soybean flour fermented
6   cups red pepper powder
2   cups salt
12 cups water

Put 12 cups water in a pan, and then pour the malt flour over it. Mix well. Let sit for 1/2 hour. Then add sweet rice powder, mixing well. Bake in oven at 300 degrees, in a large pot. Bake from midnight to 6:00 in the morning. Stir occasionally 2-3 times.

Take out pot, and boil it on the stove for 10 minutes. Add soybean powder and let cool. Add salt and red pepper powder. Mix well.

Let sit in the sun, put in a 1 gallon jar, and cover with cheesecloth. Sprinkle salt on top of sauce in jar. Ready to serve. Can keep for 6 months to a year.

LEMON SAUCE

1   tablespoon cornstarch
1/2 cup sugar
1   teaspoon grated lemon rind
1   cup water
2   tablespoons lemon juice
2   tablespoons butter
    pinch of salt

Cook first four ingredients, stirring until slightly thickened and clear. Remove from heat. Immediately stir in lemon juice, salt and butter. Serve warm over pudding.

HOT BEAN PASTE SAUCE

For this recipe, use 3 quarts malt flour sediment remaining after preparing "Korean Rice Punch". If you do not have sediment, process malt flour as shown below.

1   **pound malt flour**
3   **quarts water, divided**
4   **pounds sweet rice flour or wheat flour**
1/2 **cup salt**
2/3 **cup soy bean powder (fermented)**
2   **cups red pepper powder (fine), or to taste**

In large bowl, soak malt flour in 1 quart cold water for 1 hour. Separate malt from husks. Squeeze husks in the water they were soaking in; strain water, and set aside. Squeeze husks second time in 1 quart fresh water, remove; strain water and add to that already set aside. Squeeze husks third time in an additional quart fresh water. Discard husks. Strain water and add to other water set aside.

In ovenproof pot, add sweet rice or wheat flour to malt-flour water. Stir until smooth. In 300 degree oven cook for 3 hours. Cool until lukewarm or cold.

Stirring until smooth after each addition, blend in salt, soy bean powder, and red pepper.

LAMB CHOP SAUCE

5   **pieces of garlic clove**
4   **cups olive oil**
20 **1-foot long mint leaves, dried**
3   **6-inch long stemmed green garlics, dried**
1   **cup vinegar**
5   **jalapeno peppers, dried**
1   **teaspoon salt**

Wash green garlic and cut off roots. Wash mint leaves. Dry garlics, mint leaves and jalapeno peppers. Put 4 cups olive oil and vinegar in a quart bottle. Put dried mint leaves, green garlics, garlic cloves, salt, and jalapeno peppers in jar. Cover with lid. Let sit in jar for 6 weeks before using.

** To serve, pour over lamb chops.

SOYBEAN PASTE (TENJANG)

4   **quarts soy beans**
3   **quarts water**
1   **pound soy bean powder, fermented**
1   **cup salt**
1   **quart water**

Soak soybeans for seven hours in water. Rinse the soybeans. In a large pan boil 3 quarts of water and soy beans on high for one hour. Reduce temperature to low and cook for four hours. Let cool for thirty minutes. Drain remaining water. Combine salt, water, and soybean paste in mixing bowl. Mix on medium speed until beans are broken and mixture is smooth.

Place Tenjang in a one gallon glass jar and cover with a cheesecloth. Place a large rubberband over the mouth of the jar and the cheesecloth. Store at room temperature.

Allow the Tenjang to ferment for one month.

Side Dishes

SAUTÉED BEAN SPROUTS

2   **pounds soy bean sprouts**
2   **tablespoons sesame oil**
1   **tablespoon soy sauce**
1   **teaspoon garlic powder**
2   **cups water**

Mix sprouts, sesame seed oil, soy sauce, and garlic powder in a large pot or skillet. Sauté for 5 minutes. Add 2 cups water. Cover and cook for 5-10 minutes, depending on desired texture of vegetable.

SAUTÉED STRING BEANS

1   **pound string beans**
1/2   **teaspoon garlic salt**
2   **ounces butter**

Clean and snap off ends of the string beans. Boil beans for 5 minutes and rinse in cold water. Sauté beans with butter and garlic salt until tender.

FRIED TOFU SLICES

14   **ounces regular firm Tofu**
1/3   **cup soy sauce**
1/4   **teaspoon sesame seeds (roasted)**

Cut tofu in 1/2 to 3/4 inch slices. Heat enough sesame or vegetable oil to barely cover bottom of skillet. Fry tofu under low temperature until golden brown on both sides. Do not overcook.

Mix sesame seeds and soy sauce. To eat, dip tofu sticks into sauce. Serve with rice.

FRIED NAPA CABBAGE

2   **cups flour**
3   **cups water**
1/4   **teaspoon salt**
1   **tablespoon oil, per leaf**
1   **napa cabbage, 6 inch-long leaves**

Mix flour, water and salt in a bowl. Take a cabbage leaf and dunk it in the batter. Put oil in frying pan and heat for 5 minutes. Put cabbage leaf in and fry on medium heat to a golden brown.

Each time you fry a leaf, add 1 tablespoon of oil.

FRIED ZUCCHINI

5   zucchini, unpeeled
     salt
     flour for coating zucchini
5   eggs (optional)
2   cups flour (batter)
2   cups water (batter)
     olive or vegetable oil for frying

Cut washed zucchini into 1/2 inch slices. Place in bowl. Lightly sprinkle with salt; stir. After 20 minutes, rinse and drain. Coat zucchini with flour. (Optional: dip floured vegetable into lightly beaten eggs.)

Prepare batter by combining flour and water. (To prevent lumping, add water slowly to flour, stirring constantly). Dip zucchini in batter. Heat enough oil to just cover bottom of frying pan. Cook zucchini at medium temperature until golden brown, approximately 2 minutes on each side.

(Zucchini will be crunchy. Adjust cooking time for desired texture of vegetable.)

BREAKFAST MEAT PATTIES

1   pound ground sirloin
7   ounces regular firm tofu
3   eggs
3   green onions, with tops
1/2   teaspoon sesame seeds (roasted)
1/2   teaspoon sesame oil
1/4   teaspoon soy sauce
1/4   teaspoon garlic powder
1/2   teaspoon salt
1/4   teaspoon black pepper

Mince green onions. Combine with all other ingredients in bowl. Mix well. Form small patties (approximately 1 and 1/2 inches in diameter).

Heat enough vegetable oil to just cover bottom of skillet. Fry patties at medium temperature until brown on both sides.

BLACK BEANS (JUNG JO DUM)

2   cups black beans
1/3   cup soy sauce
1/8   cup sesame oil
1   teaspoon sugar (optional, or to taste)

Wash beans and drain (you may wish to pick out broken beans at this time), and cover beans with water and soak for 1 hour. Boil for 10 minutes and drain. Add soy sauce. Stirring constantly, dry beans over very low heat. Beans will wrinkle, with a raisin like appearance. Pour beans in bowl. Mix in sesame oil and sugar. Serve with steamed short-grain rice.

Soybeans can be substituted for black beans or the two items can be mixed.

BOILED PORK FEET (TWAEJI)

8   pigs feet
2   quarts water

Boil pigs feet for a half hour. Wash and clean them well.

4   quarts water
1/2 cup ginger
1   cup garlic
1   cup soy sauce

Mix all ingredients with the pigs feet and boil on high for one hour, then boil on low for two hours.

OPTIONAL SAUCE:

1/2 cup soy sauce
1/2 cup vinegar

This sauce may be used as a dip for the pork.

ZUCCHINI PANCAKES

4   medium zucchini's
1/2 medium yellow onion
1   teaspoon salt
2 1/2 cups flour
3   cups water

Cut zucchini in half, thinly slice halves lengthwise, and then sliver (each piece). Cut onion in half and thinly slice. Mix first 3 ingredients in bowl, and set aside for at least 10 minutes. Drain and rinse in colander to remove as much salt as possible. Set aside.

Put flour in large bowl. Mix in water one cup at a time, stirring well after each addition to remove lumps. Add zucchini and onion.

Heat 1 tablespoon of oil in a 12 inch skillet. Put in a 1/2 cup mixture, forming round pancakes. Fry 5 minutes on each side, or until golden brown.

FRIED CUTTLEFISH

8   ounces dried shredded squid (cuttlefish)
1   teaspoon garlic powder
2   tablespoons soy sauce
3   teaspoons sesame oil
1   tablespoon sesame seeds (roasted)
2   tablespoons hot red bean paste
1   teaspoon sugar
1/2 cup water
2   teaspoons hot pepper powder

Combine garlic powder, soy sauce, sesame seed oil, sesame seeds, hot pepper paste, sugar, water and hot pepper powder. In a large pan boil all the ingredients except the cuttlefish for 3 minutes. Remove from heat and mix.

FRIED POTATOES WITH FISH CAKES

5   medium white potatoes
2   cups water, divided
1   pound fresh or frozen fish cakes
1   medium yellow onion
5   green onions
1/3 cup soy sauce
1   teaspoon sesame oil
2   teaspoons sesame seeds (roasted)
1/2 teaspoon garlic powder
1/2 teaspoon red pepper powder
1   teaspoon sugar (optional)

Wash, peel, and cut potatoes in 3/4 inch cubes. In a large pot, bring 2 cups water to boil; add potatoes and soy sauce. Under low heat and stirring frequently, cook for 10 minutes.

Add all other ingredients. Under low heat and stirring occasionally, cook for an additional 10 minutes. Serve. Usually served with rice.

FRIED POTATOES WITH GREEN ONIONS

1   large potato, cut like french fries
5   green onions
1   cup cornstarch
1   cup flour
3/4 cup water
1   teaspoon salt
2   cups oil
3   pieces dried seaweed

Mix cornstarch, flour, water and salt in a bowl. Mix well. Cut green onions and potatoes. Set side.

Heat 2 cups oil in frying pan. Mix vegetables with batter. Crumble seaweed and add to batter. Drop tablespoon portions in oil. Fry each side for approximately 2 minutes.

Check potatoes to see when cooked. Serve.

EGG FOO YUNG

1   8 ounce can bean sprouts
1   6 1/8 ounce can tuna
5   green onions, with tops
5   eggs
1/8 teaspoon garlic powder

Drain sprouts and tuna, discarding liquid. Cut onions into 2 inch pieces, and then slice pieces lengthwise. Mix together all ingredients.

Heat 12 inch skillet with enough oil to barely cover bottom of pan. Put in 2 heaping teaspoons of mixture, forming a round pancake. Fry until golden brown on both sides.

STEAMED EGGS

5   eggs
2   green onions, with tops
1   teaspoon sesame seeds, crushed (roasted)
1/4 teaspoon salt, or to taste
1/4 teaspoon pepper, or to taste

Mince green onions. Beat eggs well in small bowl. Add onions, sesame seeds, salt, and pepper. Mix well. Pour mixture in top portion of double boiler. Bring water to boil. Cover and steam over boiling water for approximately 20 minutes, or until eggs are firm.

If do not have double boiler, put metal or other heatproof bowl in larger pan with one-inch of water on bottom. Bring water to boil, cover and steam, as above.

GYINIP

1   cup sesame seed leaves
2   green onions
1/2 teaspoon sugar
1/2 teaspoon garlic powder
1   teaspoon sesame oil
1   tablespoon sesame seeds (roasted)
2   tablespoons hot pepper powder
1   cup soy sauce

Mince green onions. Combine soy sauce, hot pepper powder, sesame seeds, sesame seed oil, garlic powder, sugar, and green onions. In a large pan layer the leaves. Then pour a small portion over this layer, put another layer down and pour mixture, etc. Do this until all leaves are used. Pour the remainder of the sauce over the sesame seed leaves. Boil for 20 minutes. Serve as a side dish with rice.

KOREAN DUMPLINGS

2   cups flour
6   cups water
1/4 teaspoon salt
1   tablespoon Myulchi Dashido soup stock
1/4 teaspoon crushed garlic
2   green onions (cut into 2 inch sections)
2   cups zucchini (sliced into Julienne strips)

Bring water to a boil, add soup stock and garlic. Mix 1 cup water, 2 cups flour, and 1/4 teaspoon salt. Form 1" dumplings and drop dumplings into boiling water. Stir to keep from sticking to side of pan. Boil for 5 minutes. Add zucchini and onions, boil for additional 5 minutes. Serves 3-4 People.

HOT FLAVORED PICKLED NAPA CABBAGE
(KIM CHEE)

(See color photograph.)

30	heads (approximately 45 pounds) Napa cabbage
6	quarts water
5	cups salt, divided
3	large daikon radishes
8	bunches green onions, with tops
1/8	cup ginger (approximately 3 ounces)
7	cloves garlic
3	cups hot red pepper powder
1/2	cup sugar
2	cups salted baby shrimp
5	1 gallon glass jars

Cut each head of cabbage into quarters. Stir water with 3 cups salt in large pan. Submerge each piece of cabbage in salt water solution for 3 seconds. Then place cabbage in large pan. Layer cabbage and sprinkle between layers with remaining 2 cups salt. Allow cabbage to stand for 9-10 hours. Rotate the bottom layer to the top, and let stand for 9-10 more hours.

Tip: Test for completion of the salting process by pinching together a piece of the white center section. If the portion bends without cracking, proceed to the next step. If the portion breaks, then allow the cabbage to stand until center section bends. Rinse each piece of cabbage in large bowl of water. Repeat 2 more times. Drain and set aside.

Cut radish into 4 inch pieces; sliver each piece lengthwise. Cut green onions into 2 inch pieces. Crush ginger and garlic separately. Combine red pepper and radishes; mix thoroughly. Add onions, ginger, garlic, sugar, and shrimp. Mix well. Coat each leaf with approximately 1 tablespoon radish mixture. Continue this process until all leaves have been coated.

Allow Kim Chee to ripen at room temperature for 24 hours. Refrigerate. After 1 week, the Kim Chee is ready to eat. Store in refrigerator up to 3 months.

PORK BUNS

1	loaf frozen bread dough
1	pound ground pork
1	yellow onion (minced)
5	green onions (minced)
1/4	teaspoon black pepper
1/2	teaspoon salt
1/4	teaspoon garlic powder
1/4	teaspoon soy sauce
1/4	teaspoon sugar (optional)
1/2	head cabbage (minced)
	Steamer

Mix all ingredients together.

Roll frozen bread dough into four inch wide flat pancakes. Fill with two tablespoons of filling. Pull up sides, one at a time, making sure there are no holes in the dough. Give top a twist and smooth into a round ball.

Steam buns in steamer for about twenty minutes. Let buns set for ten minutes.

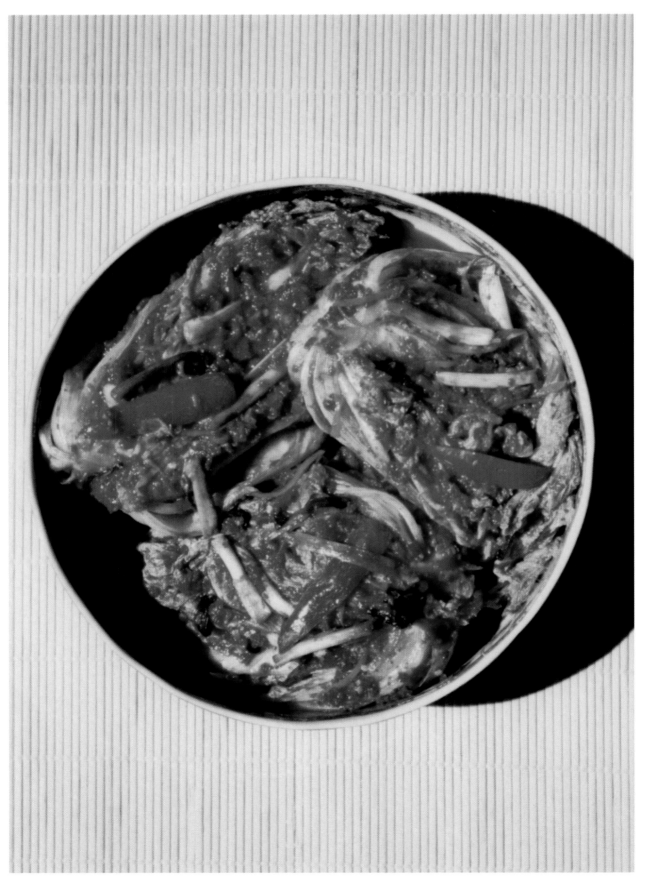

KIM CHEE

SIMPLE KIM CHEE

8   cups napa cabbage (2 inch pieces)
1/2 cup salt
1   tablespoon crushed garlic
1/2 cup crushed red peppers
1/4 teaspoon crushed ginger
5   bunches green onions
1   tablespoon salted baby shrimp
1   tablespoon sugar
1/2 cup water
1   gallon glass jar or two 1/2 gallon glass jars or four quart jars

Put a layer of cabbage into a large bowl, sprinkle with salt, continue layering cabbage with salt until last layer is salted. Set aside for 1 hour. Turn over entire amount and let set aside for 1 more hour. Test by bending. If cabbage is done it will be flexible. If not, let the cabbage set for 1/2 hour. Check in 1/2 hour intervals until the cabbage is bendable.

Wash well. Drain in strainer. Wash 5 times in a row. Put cabbage back into the bowl with garlic, pepper and ginger.

Split and cut green onions into 2 inch pieces. Mix green onions, sugar and shrimp with cabbage and spices. Add 1/2 cup water. Mix.

Stuff mixture into a glass jar and leave 2 inches at the top of the glass jar. Cover with lid.

Allow Kim Chee to ripen at room temperature for 24 hours. Refrigerate. After 1 week, the Kim Chee is ready to eat. Store in refrigerator up to 3 months.

RADISH AND PUMPKIN KIM CHEE

1   quart fresh pumpkin
1   quart daikon radish
2   fresh pollack fish heads
5   green onions
1   tablespoon garlic
1/2 cup crushed hot red peppers
1/3 cup salt
1   tablespoon sugar
1   tablespoon salted baby shrimp

Rinse fish heads and cut into quarters. Wash, peel, and cut pumpkin into squares of 1 inch by 1/4 inch thick. Wash and cut radish in the same dimensions as the pumpkin. Combine radish, pumpkin, and fish heads in large bowl. Sprinkle 1/6 cup of salt evenly over the mixture. Let the mixture set for 1/2 hour.

Rinse the radish, pumpkin and fish head mixture thoroughly and set aside. Chop green onions into 2 inch pieces and crush garlic. Combine in bowl green onions, garlic, crushed red pepper, baby shrimp, sugar, and the remainder of salt. Then mix.

Combine pumpkin, radish and fish with the seasonings. Then mix.

Put mixture in one gallon jar, cover and let stand for 24 hours at room temperature. Refrigerate. Refrigerate for 2 weeks before eating.

WHITE KIM CHEE

1   **head napa cabbage**
3   **quarts water**
1/2   **cup salt**
3   **tablespoons cornstarch**
3   **green onions**
2   **tablespoons ginger**
3   **tablespoons garlic**
1   **tablespoon sugar**
2   **red hot peppers**
1   **glass gallon jar**

Slice cabbage into 2 inch squares. Mix 2 quarts of water with 1/2 cup salt water solution for one hour. Rinse cabbage thoroughly, then set aside and allow to drain.

Boil 3 cups of water. Dissolve 3 tablespoons cornstarch in one cup of cold water. Slowly pour the cornstarch solution into the boiling water. Decrease temperature to low and let boil for five minutes. Cool for 30 minutes.

Slice green onions, ginger, and garlic into 1 inch strips. Quarter and remove the seeds from the red peppers.

Combine in large bowl: cornstarch solution, cabbage, green onions, garlic, ginger, sugar and hot peppers. Place mixture into one gallon jar. Allow to ripen at room temperature for 24 hours. Refrigerate and allow to ripen for one week. Then the white Kim Chee is ready to eat. Store in refrigerator up to one month.

STEAMED BEANCAKE WITH KIM CHEE

28   **ounces beancake**
3   **cups Kim Chee, chopped**
1   **tablespoon sesame seeds (roasted)**
1   **tablespoon sesame oil**
1/4   **teaspoon garlic powder**
1/4   **teaspoon sugar**

Chop Kim Chee and mix with sesame seeds and oil, garlic powder and sugar. Set aside. Steam beancakes with 3 cups water for 10 minutes, or until hot.

Place beancakes on platter and cover with Kim Chee sauce. Serve. Serves 2 people.

SAUTÉED KIM CHEE WITH STEAMED RICE

4   **cups steamed rice**
3   **cups chopped Kim Chee**
1/2   **teaspoon sesame oil**
1   **tablespoon sesame seeds (roasted)**
2   **green onions, chopped**
1   **teaspoon white sugar**

Optional:
1/2   **teaspoon hot paste**

Sauté Kim Chee and all ingredients except rice for approximately 5 minutes on low heat.

Add rice and sauté for approximately 5 more minutes. Ready to serve. Serves 3 people.

EGGROLLS

1 pound ground beef
1/2 pound ground pork
1 yellow onion
1 cabbage
3 green onions
1 tablespoon sesame oil
2 tablespoon sesame seeds (roasted)
1/2 teaspoon salt
1 teaspoon garlic powder
1/2 teaspoon black pepper
1/2 teaspoon sugar (optional)
4 packages square egg roll wrappers
  vegetable oil

Mince cabbage and onions. Heat empty pan for three minutes on medium heat. Pour 1 tablespoon sesame seed oil into hot pan. Then add onions, cabbage, sesame seeds, salt, garlic powder, and pepper. Saute for 10 minutes. Saute ground beef and pork for 10 minutes. Drain fat from ground beef and pork. Mix all ingredients together, and let cool for a half hour.

Place one tablespoon of fillings diagonally on egg roll wrapper and fold corner over filling. Fold up both sides. Moisten edges of last flap. Roll over until flap is completely wound around. Seal with water.

Fry egg rolls in 2 tablespoons of oil until golden brown.

VEGETARIAN EGGROLLS

4 packages square egg roll wrappers
1/2 teaspoon sugar (optional)
1 cup cabbage, finely minced
1/2 medium yellow onion
2 green onions, minced
1 tablespoon sesame oil
2 tablespoons sesame seeds (roasted)
1/2 teaspoon salt
1 teaspoon garlic powder
1/2 teaspoon black pepper

Mince cabbage and onions. Heat empty pan for three minutes on medium heat. Pour 1 tablespoon sesame seed oil into hot pan. Then add onions, cabbage, sesame seeds, salt, garlic powder, and pepper. Saute for 10 minutes. Let mixture cool for half hour.

(Refer to the first egg roll recipe for instructions on how to finish egg rolls).

CHICKEN EGGROLLS

1	pound chicken breast, chopped
1	medium cabbage, minced
1	medium yellow onion, chopped
2	tablespoons sesame oil
1/2	teaspoon garlic, chopped
2	tablespoons sesame seeds (roasted)
1	tablespoon sugar
1/2	teaspoon black pepper
1/2	teaspoon soy sauce
20-30	eggroll wrappers

Optional:

1	teaspoon salt

Mince cabbage very fine. Chop onions. Put 2 tablespoons sesame oil in a pan. Add chicken, garlic and onions. Saute for 10 minutes on low heat. Put in another bowl. Saute cabbage for 10 minutes

Mix cabbage with chicken and onions. Add seasonings. Add salt to taste. Mix well before wrapping.

(Refer to the first eggroll recipe for instructions on how to roll eggrolls.)

Roll 1 tablespoon of mixture in each eggroll skin. Fry eggrolls in 1/2 cup preheated oil. Serve.

TURKEY EGGROLLS

1	pound ground turkey
1	medium cabbage, minced
1	medium yellow onion, chopped
2	tablespoons sesame oil
1/2	teaspoon garlic, chopped
2	tablespoons sesame seeds (roasted)
1	tablespoon sugar
1/2	teaspoon black pepper
1/2	teaspoon soy sauce
20-30	eggroll wrappers

Optional:

1	teaspoon salt

Mince cabbage very fine. Chop onions. Put 2 tablespoons sesame oil in a pan. Add turkey, garlic and onions. Saute for 10 minutes on low heat. Put in another bowl. Saute cabbage for 10 minutes

Mix cabbage with turkey, garlic and onions. Add seasonings. Add salt to taste. Mix well before wrapping.

(Refer to the first eggroll recipe for instructions on how to roll eggrolls.)

Roll one tablespoon of mixture in each eggroll skin. Fry eggrolls in 1/2 cup preheated oil. Serve.

POT STICKERS

1 pound ground beef
1 pound bean sprouts
1 package fresh tofu
1 medium yellow onion
2 green onions, with tops
1/2 pound ground pork
2 eggs
2 teaspoons sesame seeds (roasted)
1 teaspoon garlic salt
1 teaspoon black pepper
1 teaspoon soy sauce
2 teaspoons sesame oil
12 ounce package round pasta wraps for pot stickers

Bring 3 quarts water to boil in large pan. Wash sprouts and throw out bad pieces. Boil 10 minutes, drain, and mince. Put sprouts and tofu into cheesecloth bag, twisting opening to be sure mixture is contained. Squeeze out water by putting bag in sink and placing large pan of water on top. (Weight of water will press out moisture). Chop yellow onions finely, and saute in dry pan for 5 minutes; mince green onions.

In large bowl, thoroughly mix all ingredients, except pop sticker wraps. Mixture should be dry to prevent wrappers from dissolving.

To make pot stickers, lay 1 wrapper on ceramic dish. Fold over to form half rounds. Starting from the center, pinch the wrapper closed, making sure all the air is removed. (Removing the air is very important; if air remains in pot sticker, the sticker will burst open during frying and possibly explode. Until you are experienced in sealing stickers, you may wish to test fry 2-3 to be sure your procedure is correct). For an especially attractive pot sticker, pleat the edges after it is sealed. Set formed pop stickers on lightly floured cookie sheet until read for frying.

Heat 1 tablespoon oil in 12-14 inch skillet. Fry pot stickers 1 inch apart for about 5 minutes on each side, or until golden brown.

VEGETARIAN POT STICKERS

16 cups water
2 cups yellow onions (minced)
2 cups bean sprouts
14 ounce package firm tofu
1 tablespoon sesame seeds (roasted)
1 tablespoon sesame oil
1/2 teaspoon soy sauce
1/2 teaspoon crushed fresh garlic or powdered garlic
1/2 teaspoon salt, or to taste
1/4 teaspoon black pepper
1 cup minced green onions, including tops
1 package round pasta egg roll wrappers
1/2 cup vegetable oil (for frying)

Bring 8 cups of water to a boil. Clean cabbage and cut into 4 parts. Boil cabbage 10 minutes. Rinse and drain cabbage in cold water. Mince and dry cabbage.

Bring 8 cups of water to a boil. Cook bean sprouts for 10 minutes. Rinse and drain bean sprouts in cold water. Mince and dry bean sprouts.

Put tofu into cheesecloth and squeeze out all the water. Mix all ingredients together. This mixture should be dry to prevent wrappers from dissolving.

(Refer to the first pot sticker recipe for instructions on how to finish pot stickers).

KIM'S TEMPURA

1 cup flour
1 cup cornstarch
1-1/2 teaspoon salt
2 cups water
2 carrots
2 white potatoes
1 sweet potato
1 yellow onion
1 bunch green onions

Mix flour, cornstarch and salt and gradually add water. The consistency should be like pancake batter.

Cut potatoes into the size of two inch long french fries. Cut green onions into two inch pieces. Cut yellow onion into slivers. Cut carrots into the size of two inch long french fries.

Mix all vegetables with batter. Deep fry in hot oil for about five minutes or until golden brown. Serve.

FRIED TEMPURA AND SPINACH SUSHI

6 ounces fish tempura
1/4 teaspoon soy sauce
1/2 teaspoon sesame seeds (roasted)
1/4 teaspoon garlic powder
1/2 teaspoon sesame oil
1/2 teaspoon sugar

Cut tempura into 1/4-inch thick slices. Put tempura, soy sauce, sesame seeds, garlic powder, sesame oil and sugar in a frying pan. Mix. Fry tempura for 5 minutes. Set aside.

Spinach:

1/2 teaspoon sesame oil
1 bundle spinach, with top chopped off
1/2 teaspoon sesame seeds (roasted)
1/4 teaspoon garlic powder
1/4 teaspoon soy sauce
1/4 teaspoon black pepper
1/4 teaspoon salt
8 cups water
steamed rice

Boil 8 cups water. Cook spinach for 5 minutes. Rinse with cold water and dry.

Mix all ingredients together in a bowl. Set aside. Put a piece of dried seaweed on a bamboo sushi roller. Spread about 1 cup of steamed rice on seaweed wrapper, leaving approximately 1 inch of wrapper at one end, uncovered. Place 2 pieces of spinach, 2 pieces of tempura and 2 pieces of pickled radish on rice. Use sushi roller to help roll up tight. Then slice sushi roll about 1/2-inch thick. Serve.

TIP: Sesame seed oil can be used to help in the cutting of the sushi roll by brushing some oil on the knife and also on the roll. It makes it easier to slice and also adds flavor.

AVOCADO AND CRAB MEAT SUSHI

 12 ounces crab meat
  2 avocados, sliced
     steamed rice

Put a piece of dried seaweed on a bamboo sushi roller. Put about 1 cup of steamed rice on the dried seaweed wrapper. Spread out evenly, but leave approximately 1 inch of wrapper at one end, uncovered. Line up 2 pieces of avocado on rice. Then 2 pieces crab meat, 2 pieces avocado, and 2 pieces crab meat. Roll up, using sushi roller to help make it tight. Then slice sushi roll about 1/2-inch thick. Serve. *See TIP, next column.

VEGETARIAN SUSHI

  2 ounces pickled radish (daikon)
  5 carrots
  1 bundle celery
  1 tablespoon sesame seeds (roasted)
 1/2 teaspoon sesame oil
 1/4 teaspoon soy sauce
 1/4 teaspoon garlic powder
  3 green onions, chopped
  1 teaspoon salt
 16 cups water, divided
     steamed rice

Boil 8 cups water. Cook celery for 5 minutes. Rinse with cold water and drain. Cut in long, thin slices. Boil 8 cups water again and cook carrots for 10 minutes. Rinse with cold water. Let cool, then slice 7 inches long, 1/4-inch thick. Mix all ingredients except pickled radish, celery and carrots together. Set aside.

Slice radish 7 inches long and 1/4-inch thick. Put a piece of dried seaweed on a bamboo sushi roller. Spread about 1 cup of steamed rice over wrapper, leaving approximately 1 inch of wrapper at one end, uncovered. Line up 2 pieces of carrot, 2 pieces of celery and 2 pieces of pickled radish. Roll up, using sushi roller to help make tight. Then slice sushi roll about 1/2-inch thick. Serve. *See TIP, next column.

RAW OYSTERS

  2 cups radish (daikon)
  8 ounces raw oysters
 1/2 cup salt
 1/2 cup soy sauce
 1/2 cup vinegar
  1 tablespoon crushed sesame seed (roasted)
  2 green onions, minced
 1/2 teaspoon sugar
 1/4 teaspoon crushed garlic

Shred 2 cups radish. Sprinkle 1/2 cup salt on oysters. Leave 10 minutes, then rinse well. Drain well. Place radish on serving dish, then arrange oysters on shredded radish. Sprinkle green onion over oysters.

Sauce:

Mix soy sauce, vinegar, sesame seeds, sugar and garlic. To eat, dip oysters in sauce.

* TIP: Sesame seed oil can be used to help in the cutting of the sushi roll by brushing some oil on the knife and also on the roll. It makes it easier to slice and also adds flavor.

KOREAN STYLE PICKLED SQUID

3   pounds frozen or fresh squid
4   cups salt, divided

In a bowl, mix squid and 2 cups salt. Put in jar and cover tightly. Store in cool place for 1 week. Strain in colander to remove accumulated liquid. Put squid in bowl; mix with an additional 2 cups salt and return to jar. Store in cool place for at least 1 month.

3   pounds pickled squid
8   jalapeno peppers
5   green onions
1   tablespoon garlic
1   tablespoon ginger
1   tablespoon sesame seeds (roasted)
1/2 cup red hot pepper powder

Rinse and drain squid. Slice squid into 4 pieces. Mince jalapeno peppers, green onions, crush garlic and ginger. Combine jalapeno peppers, green onions, garlic, ginger, and hot pepper powder to the pickled squid. Serve. Store in refrigerator.

SIMPLE PICKLED SQUID

2   cups salt
3   cups miniature squid
3   green onions, chopped
10 green jalapeno peepers, chopped
2   tablespoons sesame seeds (roasted)
1   tablespoon chopped garlic
1   tablespoon crushed ginger
1/2 teaspoon sugar
3   tablespoons red pepper powder
1   teaspoon salt
1/2 teaspoon black pepper

Peel skin off squid. Take insides out, and wash. Cut into bite-size pieces. Pour 2 cups of salt over squid and mix. Let sit for 2 hours. Wash salt off squid. Drain the water from the squid and set aside. Chop onion and peppers. Mix with remaining ingredients. Then add squid and mix again. Serve. This can be eaten raw if desired, or put in a jar and refrigerate for one month. Store in refrigerator.

PICKLED GREEN GARLIC

30   **green garlics (18 inches long)**
2   **cups soy sauce**
1/4 **cup sugar**
1/8 **cup vinegar**

Mix sugar, soy sauce, and vinegar in a bowl. Wash green garlics and cut off roots. Dry. Bend each garlic stem in half and tie the leaves around it in a knot. Let sit in sauce for 1 day, turning over a few times. Put pickled garlic in a jar, covering with remaining sauce.

Let sit at room temperature for the first 6 weeks and then refrigerate.

** To eat, cut to desired thickness and serve.

PICKLED GREEN GARLIC (HOT FLAVORED)

30   **green garlics (18 inches long)**
2   **cups soy sauce**
1   **cup hot paste**
1/4 **cup sugar**

Mix sugar, hot paste, and soy sauce in a bowl. Wash green garlics and cut off roots. Dry. Bend each garlic stem in half and tie the leaves around it in a knot.

Let sit in sauce for 1 day, turning over a few times. Put pickled garlic in a jar, covering with remaining sauce.

Let sit at room temperature for the first 6 weeks, then refrigerate.

** To eat, cut to desired thickness and serve.

PICKLED JALAPENO PEPPERS

Jalapeno peppers
White vinegar
2 **cups soy sauce**
4 **cups water**
1 **cup sugar**

Fill glass quart jar full with jalapeno peppers. Soak peppers in white vinegar for 2 weeks in a covered jar at room temperature. Pour out vinegar. Boil in a pan: soy sauce, water, and sugar. Cool slightly and pour over jalapeno peppers in the jar. Cover tightly with lid. Set aside at room temperature for 4 weeks.

PICKLED GARLIC

6 **pounds whole garlic cloves**
2 **quarts vinegar**
3 **quarts soy sauce**

Remove the first two layers of garlic skin. Place garlic in jar and pour two quarts of vinegar over the garlic. Cover the top of the jar with two layers of paper towels and stretch a rubber band around the neck of jar. Allow garlic to pickle for one month at room temperature.

After one month, drain the vinegar. Bring three quarts of soy sauce to a boil. Cool soy sauce, then pour the soy sauce into the jar and cover with two layers of paper towels and stretch a rubber band around the neck of the jar. Let stand for two weeks in room temperature, then refrigerate.

BOILED OYSTERS WRAPPED IN GREEN ONIONS WITH HOT SAUCE

1   cup hot paste
1   green onion, chopped
1/8   cup vinegar
1/8   cup sugar
16   ounces oysters (raw)
4   bundles green onions

Boil 1 quart of water. Wash green onions and cut off roots. Add 4 bundles of green onions and cook for 5 minutes. Drain and set aside. Boil 5 cups water. Wash oysters and then put into boiling water. Stir. Cook for 2 minutes and drain. Wrap one green onion around each oyster. Place on a platter. If desired, quarter a cucumber and serve with the oysters.

Hot Sauce:
Mix remaining ingredients in a bowl. Dip oyster rolls into sauce to eat. Goes well with Japanese Rice Wine.

SAUTÉED GREEN GARLIC

6   green garlics
1   tablespoon water
2   teaspoons soy sauce
1/2   teaspoon sesame oil
1/2   teaspoon sesame seeds (roasted)
1/2   teaspoon hot pepper powder
1/4   teaspoon sugar

Wash green garlics, cut off roots and dry. Cut into 2-inch long sections and cut each section in half lengthwise. Sauté in 1 tablespoon water, for 2 minutes on low heat. Mix green garlic with remaining ingredients. Serve.

BOILED LEEK WITH HOT SAUCE

2   leeks
1   cup hot paste
1   green onion, chopped
1/8   cup vinegar
1/8   cup sugar

Cut leek into four sections. Cut off roots. Wash well. Boil in 5 cups water for 5 minutes, stirring occasionally. Strain, but don't rinse. Take a few pieces and wrap then in a ball. Place leeks on a platter.

Hot Sauce: Mix the remaining ingredients in a bowl. Put in a small serving bowl. Dunk leek in sauce to eat.

DEEP-FRIED SHRIMP

1   **cup cornstarch**
1   **cup flour**
3/4   **cup water**
1   **teaspoon salt**
15   **pieces shrimp (raw)**
2   **cups vegetable oil**

Mix cornstarch, flour, water and salt in a bowl. Mix well. Peel shrimp and wash. Cut in half. Put 1/2 cup flour on a plate. Put meat on plate also. Rub in flour.

Heat 3 cups oil in a frying pan. Dip flour-covered shrimp in batter. Fry. To eat, dip in soy sauce.

DEEP-FRIED MINIATURE SQUID

1   **cup cornstarch**
1   **cup flour**
3/4   **cup water**
1   **teaspoon salt**
10   **pieces miniature squid (raw)**
2   **cups vegetable oil**

Mix cornstarch, flour, water and salt in a bowl. Mix well. Peel squid and wash well. Cut in fourths. Put 1/2 cup flour on a plate. Put meat on plate also. Rub in flour.

Heat 2 cups oil in a frying pan. Dip flour-covered squid in batter. Deep fry. To eat, dip in soy sauce.

KIM'S SAUTÉED MUSSELS

1/2   **pound smoked mussels (precooked)***
1   **cup soy sauce**
1/4   **cup sesame oil**
1   **cup brown sugar**

Mix soy sauce, sesame oil and brown sugar in a frying pan. Heat for 5 minutes. Add mussels, and slowly cook for 10 minutes. When color is dark brown, they are done.

***Alternative:** You can buy the black mussel shells in the store. Cook in 6 cups water for 10 minutes. Take mussels out of shells, and let drain. Then cook in pan with the sauce.

SAUTÉED ALASKA POLLACK

1   **cup water**
1/2   **teaspoon salt**
1   **tablespoon sesame seeds (roasted)**
1/4   **teaspoon soy sauce**
1   **tablespoon sesame oil**
1   **teaspoon hot pepper powder**
1/2   **teaspoon sugar**
6   **ounces dried seasoned Alaska Pollack**

Boil water, salt, sesame seeds, soy sauce, sesame seed oil, hot pepper powder and sugar for 3 minutes on high heat. Remove from heat then add Pollack and mix. Cook all ingredients on low heat for 5 minutes.

SAUTÉED POLLACK

2 ounces pollack (dried)
1 tablespoon hot paste
1/2 teaspoon garlic powder
1/2 teaspoon sesame oil
1 tablespoon sesame seeds (roasted)
1 teaspoon sugar
1 tablespoon water
3 green onions, 1-inch long

Optional:

1/4 teaspoon salt

Wash green onions and cut off roots. Mix all ingredients together except pollack and onions. Heat for 5 minutes. Then add pollack and saute for 5 more minutes. Add green onions. Serve.

KOREAN-STYLE BARBECUED SHARK FILLET

1 pound skinless, boneless shark fillet
1 1/2 cup soy sauce
1/4 teaspoon chopped garlic
1/2 teaspoon sugar
1/4 teaspoon black pepper
1 teaspoon sesame seeds (roasted)
1/2 teaspoon sesame oil
3 green onion, chopped

Wash green onions and cut bottoms off. Wash shark fillet. Dab dry with a towel. Mix all ingredients in a container. Marinate shark for 1 hour in refrigerator. Barbecue on top of aluminum foil.

OR . . . .
Bake in oven at 350 degrees for approximately 10 minutes each side. Serve with rice.

SPICY SAUTÉED MINIATURE OCTOPUS

1 tablespoon sesame seeds (roasted)
2 tablespoons hot pepper powder
1/2 cup water
1 tablespoon garlic, chopped
1 tablespoon hot paste
1/2 cabbage
1/2 yellow onion, sliced
3 green onions, 1-inch long
2 pounds miniature octopus
1 teaspoon sugar

Optional:

3 jalapeno peppers

Mix sugar, hot pepper powder, sesame seeds, water, hot paste and garlic. Stir well. Shred cabbage. Wash and cut green onions into 1-inch long pieces. Slice yellow onion. Cut octopus lengthwise and then into bite-size pieces. Heat the sauce in a frying pan on low heat, for 5 minutes. Add cabbage and onions, and sauté in sauce for 5 minutes. Then add octopus. Sauté for 5 more minutes. Ready to serve. Serve with rice.

STEAMED DUNGEONESS CRAB

3   pounds Dungeoness crab (fresh)
6   cups water
1/2 teaspoon salt

Boil salt and water in a pan. Scrub crab and wash. Add to water and cook for 10 minutes. Serves 2-3 people.

BAKED TILAPIA FISH

1-2 pounds tilapia fish
1/2 teaspoon salt, or to taste
     olive oil

Clean scales off tilapia fish. Slice fish through middle, but not all the way through. Brush olive oil onto top and bottom of fish. Put in a pan. Sprinkle salt onto top, bottom and inside of fish. Let sit in refrigerator for 1 hour. Wash well and bake.

SPICY SAUTÉED MINIATURE SQUID

1   tablespoon sesame seeds (roasted)
2   tablespoons hot pepper powder
1/2 cup water
1   tablespoon garlic, grated
1   tablespoon hot paste
1/2 cabbage
1/2 yellow onion, sliced
3   green onions, 1-inch long
2   pounds miniature squid
1   teaspoon sugar

Optional:
3   jalapeno peppers, seedless

Mix sugar, hot pepper powder, sesame seeds, water, hot paste and garlic. Stir well. Shred cabbage. Wash and cut green onions into 1-inch long pieces. Slice yellow onion. Cut squid lengthwise and then into bite-size pieces. Heat the sauce in a frying pan on low heat, for 5 minutes. Add jalapeno peppers if desired. Add cabbage and onions, and sauté in sauce for 5 minutes. Then add squid. Sauté for 5 more minutes. Ready to serve. Serve with rice.

FRIED SPANISH MACKEREL

1/4 cup salt
2   pounds Spanish mackerel (fresh)
1   cup vegetable oil

Sprinkle salt over fish and thoroughly cover. Let sit 1/2 hour. Then wash and scrape scales off. Remove stomach and clean. Fry in 1 cup oil for 2 minutes each side. Serve.

BOILED CHICKEN WITH SOY SAUCE
(DAGULGE JHIM)

3 quarts water
1/3 cup sesame oil
1 cup sugar
1 cup soy sauce
12 chicken thighs

Boil chicken in 3 quarts water, for 1/2 hour. Wash well. Set aside.

Mix soy sauce with 1/2 cup water. Then add sugar and sesame oil. Mix chicken and sauce together.

Put in a pan and cook. Boil for 10 minutes on high heat. Make sure chicken is cooked well. Strain and discard juice from chicken. Best served with steamed, short-grain rice.

FRIED CHICKEN GIZZARD

1 pound chicken gizzards
2 cups vegetable oil
   flour

Wash gizzards well. Make slice marks in each piece of gizzard, but not all the way through. Cover each piece thoroughly with flour. Fry in 2 cups cooking oil, for 5 minutes each side, or until golden brown. Serve.

BOILED CHICKEN GIZZARD

5 cups water
1/2 teaspoon salt
1 pound chicken gizzards

Wash gizzards well. Boil 5 cups water, salt and gizzards for approximately 1/2 hour. Serve.

BOILED BEEF WITH SOY SAUCE
(SOLGULGE JUNG JO DUM)

(See color photograph.)

2 pounds boneless round rump roast, or other lean boneless beef
7 cups water, divided
2 cups soy sauce
3 garlic cloves
5 tablespoons sugar, or to taste
10-15 jalapeno peppers (optional)

Wash meat and cut into 1 and 1/2 inch chunks. Bring 6 cups of water to a boil. Add beef, boil for 10 minutes and wash well a second time to thoroughly clean meat. Wash pan.

In clean pan, mix soy sauce and 1 cup of water. Add meat and boil for 1/2 hour. Peel garlic, add with sugar and, if desired, jalapeno peppers. Continue boiling for 1/2 hour. Serve with rice.

SOLGULGE JUNG JO DUM

KOREAN-STYLE BEEF WITH EGGS

2   pounds beef roast, without fat
1 1/2   cups sugar
2   cups soy sauce
10   pieces of garlic, whole
6   cups water
10   eggs

Boil 2 cups water. Add beef roast and cook for approximately 10 minutes. Wash meat well and throw away water. Cook on medium heat 6 cups water, soy sauce, sugar and beef roast for approximately 45 minutes.

Boil eggs in water for approximately 1/2 hour. Let cool and peel. Set aside. Peel garlic and add eggs and garlic to broth. Cook for 5 minutes.

Take meat out and slice to desired thickness. Take eggs out and cut in half. Put meat and eggs on a platter and serve on the side.

STEAMED BEEF MUNDU

1   pound beef cube steak
3   green onions, minced
1   6-inch long cucumber
1   tablespoon sesame seeds (roasted)
1/2   teaspoon garlic, grated
1/4   teaspoon black pepper
1/4   teaspoon soy sauce
1/4   teaspoon salt
1   teaspoon sesame oil
2   packages round egg roll skins

Mix all ingredients in a bowl, except cucumber. Cut cucumber in half. Then cut off ends of cucumber including about 1/2 inch of cucumber. Finely chop this section. Saute for 5 minutes on low temperature. Put in cheesecloth and squeeze all the juice out. Cucumber must be cooled before adding to beef.

Mix all ingredients together. Put 1 teaspoon into each round eggroll skin. Wrap up. Put 2 quarts water in a steamer. Steam mundu on high temperature for 1/2 hour. Watch water to make sure it doesn't get too low.

For a sauce you can use 1/2 cup soy sauce and 1/2 cup vinegar mixed, or just plain soy sauce.

CHAYOTE SQUASH WITH BEEF

1/4	teaspoon salt
1/2	pound beef, New York cut
1	teaspoon sesame oil
1	chayote squash
2	green onions, 1-inch long
1	teaspoon soy sauce
2	teaspoons sesame seeds (roasted)
1/2	teaspoon garlic powder
1/4	teaspoon black pepper
2	jalapeno peppers, quartered, without seeds

Saute beef in sesame oil for 5 minutes. Slice chayote squash like thin french fries. Add squash, onions and remaining ingredients to meat. Cook for 10 minutes. Add salt to taste. Serve.

CHAYOTE SQUASH WITH PORK

1/4	teaspoon salt
1/2	pound pork roast
1	teaspoon sesame oil
1	chayote squash, sliced like thin french fries
2	green onions, minced
1	teaspoon soy sauce
2	teaspoons sesame seeds (roasted)
1/2	teaspoon garlic powder
1/4	teaspoon black pepper

Wash and slice pork thinly. Sauté pork in sesame oil for 5 minutes. Then add squash and onions, and remaining ingredients. Cook for 10 minutes. Add salt to taste.

STIR-FRIED PORK WITH KIM CHEE

1	pound pork loin
2	cups Kim Chee
3	green onions including tops
3	tablespoons sesame seed oil
1/2	teaspoon black pepper
1/2	teaspoon crushed garlic
1/4	teaspoon ground chili pepper
1	teaspoon sesame seeds (roasted)

Cut pork loin into 3/16 of an inch thickness, or have a butcher cut it for you. Pre boil pork to remove excess fat. Cut green onions into 2 inch long pieces. In a frying pan heat sesame oil and add pork. Cook and stir over high heat. Season with pepper.

Squeeze liquid out of Kim Chee. Add Kim Chee to pork. Add remaining ingredients. Stir-fry briefly. Serve with steamed short grain rice.

STEAMED PORK MUNDU WITH KIM CHEE

1	pound ground pork
2	cups chopped Kim Chee, squeezed dry
2	green onions, minced
1/4	teaspoon garlic powder
1/4	teaspoon black pepper
1/2	teaspoon sesame oil
1	tablespoon sugar
2	packages round egg roll skins

Mix all ingredients together in a bowl. Add salt to taste. Put 1 teaspoon into each round eggroll skin. Wrap up and put aside. Put 2 quarts water in a steamer. Steam eggrolls on high temperature for 1/2 hour. Watch water to make sure it doesn't get too low.

For a sauce you can use 1/2 cup soy sauce and 1/2 cups vinegar mixed, or just plain soy sauce.

STEAMED VEGETARIAN KIM CHEE MUNDU

14   ounces soybean cake
2   cups chopped Kim Chee, squeezed dry
2   green onions, minced
1/4   teaspoon garlic powder
1/4   teaspoon black pepper
1/2   teaspoon sesame oil
1   tablespoon sesame seeds (roasted)
1   teaspoon sugar
1   package round egg roll skins

Squeeze the bean cake with a cheesecloth to remove all the water. Mix all ingredients in a bowl. Add salt to taste. Put 1 teaspoon into each round eggroll skin. Wrap up and put aside.

Put 2 quarts water in a steamer. Steam eggrolls on high temperature for 1/2 hour. Watch water to make sure it doesn't get too low.

For a sauce you can use 1/2 cup vinegar and 1/2 cup soy sauce mixed, or just plain soy sauce. Serve.

STEAMED VEGETARIAN MUNDU

1   English cucumber
3   green onions, minced
1   tablespoon sesame seeds (roasted)
1/2   teaspoon garlic, chopped
1/4   teaspoon black pepper
1/4   teaspoon salt
1   teaspoon sesame oil
14   ounces soybean cake
1   package round egg roll skins

Mix all ingredients except cucumbers and bean cake in a bowl. Cut cucumber into 1-inch long sections. Remove the ends of the cucumber. Chop cucumber finely. Saute for 5 minutes on low temperature. Put in cheesecloth and squeeze all the juice out. Also use cheesecloth to squeeze the juice from the bean cake. Cucumbers must be cooled before adding to beef.

Mix all ingredients together. Put 1 teaspoon into each round eggroll wrapper. Wrap up and put aside.

Put 2 quarts water in a steamer. Steam eggrolls on high temperature for 1/2 hour. Watch water to make sure it doesn't get too low.

For a sauce you can use 1/2 cup soy sauce and 1/2 cup vinegar mixed, or just plain soy sauce. Serve.

ASSORTED VEGETABLES (NAMOOL)

1   bunch spinach
1   pound soybean sprouts
1   daikon radish
1/2 pound ferns (go sa de)
4   teaspoons garlic powder (divided)
2   teaspoons salt (divided)
5   teaspoons sesame oil (divided)
2   teaspoons ground sesame seeds (roasted, divided)
4   green onions
3   teaspoons soy sauce (divided)

Wash spinach well and cook in boiling water for five minutes. Rinse in cold water and squeeze excess water from spinach. Cut spinach into two pieces. Add 1/2 teaspoon sesame seed oil, 1 teaspoon garlic powder, 1/2 teaspoon salt, 1/2 teaspoon sesame seeds and 1 minced green onion to the spinach.

Slice daikon into thin julienne strip. Saute on low heat for ten minutes. Add 1 teaspoon soy sauce, 1 teaspoon of garlic powder, 1/2 teaspoon salt, 1/2 teaspoon sesame seed oil, 1/2 teaspoon sesame seeds and 1 minced green onion.

Wash bean sprouts well and saute on low heat for ten minutes. Add 1 teaspoon soy sauce, 1 teaspoon garlic powder, 1/2 teaspoon salt, 2 teaspoons of sesame seed oil, 1/2 teaspoon sesame seeds and 1 minced green onion to the bean sprouts.

Soak ferns in hot water for five hours. Wash well. Saute with 2 teaspoons of sesame seed oil for five minutes. Add 1 teaspoon soy sauce, 1 teaspoon garlic powder, 1/2 teaspoon salt, 1/2 teaspoon sesame seeds and 1 minced green onion and saute for ten more minutes. Serve all vegetables separately.

FRIED SOYBEAN CAKE WITH HOT SAUCE

14 ounces soybean cake
2   green onions, minced
1   cup soy sauce
1   tablespoon sesame oil
1   tablespoon sesame seeds (roasted)
1   tablespoon hot chili pepper powder
1/2 teaspoon garlic powder
1/4 teaspoon sugar

Slice bean cake lengthwise, and then 1-inch thick slices across. Drain water off. Let sit for 10 minutes. Fry to a golden brown. Put on a plate. Mix remaining ingredients and pour desired amount over top. Serve.

BOILED SOYBEAN CAKE WITH HOT SAUCE

This makes an excellent midday meal.

14 ounces soybean cake
2   green onions, minced
1   cup soy sauce
1   tablespoon sesame oil
1   tablespoon sesame seeds (roasted)
1   tablespoon hot chili pepper powder
1/2 teaspoon garlic powder
1/4 teaspoon sugar

Mix all ingredients except bean cake in a bowl. Put soybean cake in a pan, with 1 cup water, and cook slowly for 10 minutes. Take soybean cake out of pan and put on a plate. Put desired amount of sauce over top. Serve.

Main Dishes

HOT BARBECUED CHICKEN

1   tablespoon White Zinfandel Wine
1/2 teaspoon chopped garlic
1/2 cup oyster sauce
1/2 cup soy sauce
1/2 cup honey
1/2 teaspoon black pepper
1   tablespoon hot paste
2   green onions, chopped
1/2 yellow onion, grated
2   chickens

Cut chicken in half. Remove skin and clean. Sprinkle lightly with salt. Bake for 10 minutes in oven, at 350 degrees.

Mix remaining ingredients in a bowl. Bake chicken for 45 minutes to 1 hour, spreading more sauce over chicken every 10 minutes. Check periodically. Serve with rice. Serves 4 people.

BARBECUED CHICKEN

2   medium chickens
1   cup worcestershire sauce
1/2 cup honey
1/2 teaspoon black pepper
1/2 teaspoon crushed ginger
1   teaspoon chopped garlic
1   tablespoon grated yellow onion
1   tablespoon White Zinfandel Wine

Optional:
1/3 cup ketchup

Mix all ingredients except chickens in a bowl. Set aside. Peel skin off chicken and wash. Put in a pan. Bake in oven for 10 minutes. Brush sauce over chicken, thoroughly. Cook for 45 minutes to 1 hour. Every 10 minutes spread more sauce over chicken until sauce is gone. Serves 4-5 people.

ALMOND CHICKEN

2 cups vegetable oil
1 medium chicken breast, sliced thin

Batter:

1/3 cup flour
1/3 cup corn starch
1 cup water
1/4 teaspoon salt

Sauce:

1 cup cold water
1/2 pound ginger, scraped and sliced thin
1 cup corn starch

Optional:

1/2 cup almonds (chopped)

Mix flour, 1 cup water, 1/3 cup corn starch and 1/4 teaspoon salt in a bowl. Put chicken in and mix. Heat 2 cups oil in frying pan. Fry chicken for approximately 2 minutes each side, or until golden brown.

Slowly boil ginger in 8 cups water for 1 hour. Strain water out. Boil ginger stock for 5 minutes. Mix cornstarch and cold water in a bowl, by lifting ginger stock juice in measuring cup and pouring back in bowl. Set aside for 10 minutes. Slowly stir in cornstarch and water to ginger stock. Cook for 5 minutes.

Put chicken on a platter and pour the sauce over the chicken. Top with 1/2 cup chopped almonds. Serve.

BARBECUED CHICKEN WINGS

5 cups chicken wings, cut in three
1 cup soy sauce
1/2 cup sugar
1 teaspoon black pepper
1 tablespoon sesame oil
1 tablespoon sesame seeds (roasted)
1 tablespoon chopped garlic
1/2 teaspoon hot paste

Mix all ingredients except chicken in a container. Cut chicken wings in three. Add to sauce.

Let sit for 1 day, turning over periodically.

Bake or barbecue. If baked in oven, cook at 350 degrees for approximately 1/2 hour. Check chicken with a fork. Serve.

LEMON CHICKEN

2	cups vegetable oil
5	cups chicken breast
1	cup flour
1	cups cornstarch
1/2	teaspoon salt
1	cup water
2	cups lemon sauce

Mix flour, cornstarch, salt and water in a bowl. Put chicken in and mix. Heat oil in frying pan, and deep fry chicken approximately 2 minutes each side, or until golden brown. Put chicken on a platter.

Heat 2 cups lemon sauce and pour over chicken. Optional: Add 1 teaspoon sugar, or to desired taste. Serve with rice. Serves 4-5 people.

SAUTEÉD CHICKEN AND VEGETABLES

3	pounds chicken breast
1/2	pound mushrooms, sliced
1	yellow onion, sliced
7	cups celery, sliced
1/2	pound pea pods
1/2	pound bean sprouts
3	cups cabbage, sliced
2	medium tomatoes, quartered
5	green onions, cut into 2-inch long pieces
1/2	cup flour or cornstarch
1	tablespoon salt
1/2	teaspoon garlic powder
1	tablespoon hot paste
1/2	teaspoon black pepper

Cut yellow onion and bell pepper in half and slice. Slice mushrooms. Quarter tomatoes. Cut celery slightly diagonally into approximately 1-inch long sections. Cut cabbage in half and then slice into 1/2-inch thick slices.

Boil 6 cups water and add mushrooms. Let cook for a few seconds, take out and rinse with cold water. Wash peas and set aside. Put bean sprouts in 6 cups water and boil for a few seconds. Take out, rinse with cold water and set aside. Boil 6 cups water again and add yellow onion, green onions, bell pepper, celery, pea pods and cabbage. Boil for a few seconds, take out and rinse. Set aside.

Boil 3 new cups of water. Remove 1 cup and put in a bowl, but keep remaining 2 cups water boiling. Mix the 1 cup water with flour or cornstarch. Add mixture slowly to the 2 boiling cups of water and stir. Add black pepper, hot paste, garlic powder and salt. Cook for 5 minutes on low heat.

Meanwhile, boil chicken in 5 cups water for about 10 minutes, to remove blood. Rinse off chicken. Remove skin from chicken and strip into bite size pieces. Boil in 10 cups water again for about 45 minutes to 1 hour. Chicken will be rubbery if not cooked all the way.

Add chicken and cooked vegetables to sauce in pan. Mix and serve with rice. Serves 4-5 people.

KIM'S SWEET AND SOUR CHICKEN
(KOREAN STYLE)

1   pound whole chicken wings
2   yellow onions (cut into medium pieces)
1   red bell pepper (sliced very thin)
1   cucumber (striped and sliced thin)
2   carrots (striped and sliced thin)
1   teaspoon salt
1   teaspoon cornstarch
2   teaspoons sugar
    Vegetable oil
    Vinegar
    Soy sauce

Batter:

1   cup flour
1   cup cornstarch
1-1/2 teaspoons salt
2   cups water

Batter: Mix one cup of four, one cup of cornstarch, one and half teaspoons of salt and water in a large bowl. The consistency should be like pancake batter.

Cut chicken wings into two parts. Set tips aside. Dip the wings into the batter and deep fry until golden brown. Take tips and boil on high for a half hour in eight cups of water. This is to be used for the sweet and sour sauce. Remove tips and add cornstarch, sugar, salt and cook on high heat for about five minutes. The sauce should be thick by now. Add vegetables and mix well. Pour sauce over chicken wings.

For a dip, mix 1 part soy sauce with 1 part vinegar. Serves 3-4 people.

CHICKEN BULKOGEE

5   cups chicken breast
1   cup soy sauce
1/2 cup water
1/2 cup sugar
1/8 cup sesame oil
2   tablespoons sesame seeds (roasted)
1   tablespoon chopped garlic
2   green onions, chopped
1   teaspoon black pepper

Cut chicken breast into thin slices. Put in a container. Mix remaining ingredients in a bowl. Pour over chicken and mix. Spread out in container. Let sit for 1 day, turning every 5-6 hour.

When barbecued, put tin foil on rack, and chicken on top of foil. This makes the meat stay moist. Serve with steamed short grain rice. Serves 4-5 people.

POTATO DUMPLINGS WITH CHICKEN BROTH

1   cup grated potatoes
2   cups flour
8   cups chicken broth
3   green onions, chopped
2   zucchini, cut in half and sliced
1   teaspoon garlic powder
1   teaspoon salt
1/2 chicken

Cook chicken in 5 cups water, for 5 minutes. Wash chicken off, and throw away water. On high heat cook chicken again in 10 cups water, for 1/2 hour. Take chicken out and save 8 cups of chicken broth. Set aside.

Peel potatoes and grate. Put in a bowl. Add 1 1/2 cups flour. Knead for 20 minutes. Gradually add the remaining 1/2 cup of flour. It is done if, when you poke it, it doesn't bounce back out. Set aside.

Bring chicken broth to a boil. Take a little bowl with water and moisten fingertips. Tear dough into bite-size pieces and drop into broth. Cook. Done when dumplings rise to the top. Add garlic, salt, onions and zucchini. Cook for 5 minutes. Turn off heat and let sit for 5 minutes. Add salt to taste. Serve.

KOREAN CHICKEN FLAVORED DUMPLINGS

2   cups flour
1   cup cold water
1/2 teaspoon salt
2   small potatoes, cubed
2   green onions, chopped
1   teaspoon garlic
1   quart chicken broth
1   quart water
2   tablespoons sesame seeds (roasted)

Boil 1 quart water. Add potatoes and soup stock. Boil for 10 minutes. Mix flour and salt in large bowl. Gradually add 1 cup cold water. Knead. It is done if, when you poke it, it doesn't bounce back. Split dough in half. Wet finger tips. Pull off bite-size pieces of dough and drop into soup.

Cook for 10 minutes. Stir occasionally. Turn off heat. Add green onions. Let sit for 5 minutes before serving. Serve.

BARBECUED CORNISH HENS

2   green onions, chopped
1/4   cup oyster sauce
1/4   cup worcestershire sauce
1/4   cup soy sauce
1/4   cup honey
1/2   teaspoon black pepper
1/2   teaspoon garlic, chopped
1   tablespoon sesame seeds (roasted)
1/2   teaspoon sesame oil
1/2   yellow onion, grated
1/8   cup sugar
2   medium Cornish hens

Cut hens in half and wash. In a large bowl mix remaining ingredients with hens. Marinate for 1 day in the refrigerator, turning over once.

Barbecue or bake. If baked, cook in oven at 350 degrees for 45 minutes. Serve with rice. Serves 4 people.

MARINATED CORNISH HENS
(HOT FLAVORED)

3   tablespoons sesame seed oil
3   tablespoons crushed sesame seeds (roasted)
2   tablespoons garlic powder
2   cups soy sauce
1/2   cup hot pepper paste (optional)
3   green onions, chopped
4   Cornish hens, halved and cleaned

Combine sesame seed oil, sesame seeds, garlic powder, soy sauce, sugar, black pepper, green onions, and hot pepper paste. Marinate Cornish hens in sauce for 8 hours in the refrigerator. Bake at 400 degrees for 10 minutes. Then decrease temperature to 300 degrees and bake for 35 minutes.

MARINATED CORNISH HENS

2   Cornish hens
1   tablespoon White Zinfandel Wine
1   tablespoon sesame seeds (roasted)
1   tablespoon sesame oil
2   tablespoons soy sauce
2   tablespoons worcestershire sauce
2   tablespoons oyster sauce
1/2   teaspoon garlic powder
1/2   teaspoon black pepper
1/2   cup honey
3   green onions, chopped
1   tablespoon sugar

Wash and clean hens. Put in plastic container. Mix remaining ingredients in a bowl and pour over hens. Mix. Let sit for 1 day in the refrigerator, turning over a few times. Barbecue or bake. If baked, cook at 350 degrees for approximately 1 hour. Ready to serve. Serves 4 people.

HOT BARBECUED QUAIL

1   tablespoon White Zinfandel Wine
4   quails, cut in half
1/2   teaspoon chopped garlic
1/2   cup oyster sauce
1/2   cup soy sauce
1/2   cup honey
1/2   teaspoon black pepper
1   tablespoon hot paste
2   green onions, chopped
1/2   yellow onion, grated

Cut quails in half. Clean and wash well. Sprinkle with salt. Mix remaining ingredients in a bowl. Put quail in a pan.

Bake at 350 degrees for 10 minutes. Spread some sauce over quails and cook for 45 minutes to 1 hour, spreading more sauce over quails every 10 minutes. Check periodically. Serve with rice. Serves 8 people.

HOT BARBECUED DUCK

1   tablespoon White Zinfandel Wine
1   duck, cut in half
1/2   teaspoon chopped garlic
1/2   cup oyster sauce
1/2   cup soy sauce
1/2   cup honey
1/2   teaspoon black pepper
1   tablespoon hot paste
2   green onions, chopped
1/2   yellow onion, grated

Cut duck in half and wash. Remove skin if desired. Sprinkle with salt. Mix remaining ingredients in a bowl. Put duck in a pan.

Bake at 350 degrees for 10 minutes. Then spread some sauce over the duck and cook for 45 minutes to 1 hour, spreading more sauce over duck every 10 minutes. Check periodically. Serve with rice. Serves 4 people.

KIM'S TURKEY MEATBALLS

5   green onions, chopped
1/2 yellow onion, chopped
2   tablespoons sesame seeds (roasted)
1   teaspoon chopped garlic
1   tablespoon sesame oil
1/2 teaspoon black pepper
1   tablespoon hot pepper powder
2   pound ground turkey
1/2 teaspoon salt
2   tablespoons vegetable oil

Optional:

2   eggs

Heat 2 tablespoons vegetable oil in a large pan. Mix all ingredients in a bowl. Make walnut-size balls and drop into pan. Fry over low heat, to golden brown. Leave in pan.

Sauce:

2   cups water
3   chicken bouillon cubes
1/2 pound fresh mushrooms
6   green onions, chopped
1/2 teaspoon sugar

Heat 2 cups water. Add bouillon cubes and dissolve. Add remaining ingredients. Boil well for 10 minutes. When done, pour over meatballs and boil for 5 more minutes. Serve with rice.

TURKEY BULKOGEE

5   cups turkey breast
1   cup soy sauce
1/2 cup water
1/2 cup sugar
1/8 cup sesame oil
2   tablespoons sesame seeds (roasted)
1   tablespoon chopped garlic
2   green onions, chopped
1   teaspoon black pepper

Cut turkey breast into thin slices. Put in a bowl. Pour over turkey and mix. Mix remaining ingredients in a bowl. Pour over turkey and mix. Spread out in container. Let sit for 1 day in the refrigerator, turning every 5-6 hours.

When barbecued, put aluminum foil on rack, and turkey on top of foil. This makes the meat stay moist. Serve with short grain rice. Serves 4-5 people.

cups water again for about 45 minutes to 1 hour. Turkey will be rubbery if not cooked all the way.

Add turkey and cooked vegetables to sauce in pan. Mix and serve with rice. Serves 4-5 people.

KOREAN-STYLE BAKED TURKEY BREAST

1	large turkey breast
1/2	cup soy sauce
2	green onions
2	teaspoons garlic powder
1/2	cup sugar
1/8	cup sesame seeds (roasted)
1	tablespoon black pepper

Cut roots off of green onions and wash. Then cut into 1-inch long pieces. Wash and remove skin from turkey. Put turkey breast on a cookie sheet and brush with sauce. Put in oven and bake at 350 degrees for approximately 1/2 hour, to a golden brown. Keep brushing with sauce until gone. Turn over once. Serves 3-4 people.

HOT BOILED TURKEY AND VEGETABLES

3	pounds turkey breast
1/2	pound mushrooms, sliced
1	yellow onion, sliced
1	bell pepper, sliced
7	cups celery, sliced
1/2	pound pea pods
1/2	pound bean sprouts
3	cups cabbage, sliced
2	medium tomatoes, quartered
5	green onions, 2-inch long pieces
1/2	cup flour or cornstarch
1	tablespoon salt
1/2	teaspoon garlic powder
1	tablespoon hot paste
1/2	teaspoon black pepper

Cut yellow onion and bell pepper in half and slice. Slice mushrooms. Quarter tomatoes. Cut celery slightly diagonally into approximately 1-inch long sections. Cut cabbage in half and then slice into 1/2-inch thick slices.

Boil 6 cups water and add mushrooms. Let sit for a few seconds, take out and rinse with cold water. Wash peas. Put bean sprouts in 6 cups water and boil for a few seconds. Take out, rinse with cold water and set aside. Boil 6 cups water again and add yellow onion, green onions, bell pepper, celery, pea pods and cabbage. Boil for a few seconds. Take out and rinse. Set aside.

Boil 3 cups water. Take out 1 cup and put it in a bowl, but keep the other 2 cups boiling. Mix the 1 cup water with flour or cornstarch. Add mixture slowly to boiling 2 cups water and stir. Add black pepper, hot paste, salt, and garlic powder. Cook for 5 minutes on low heat.

Boil turkey in 5 cups water, to get blood out for about 10 minutes. Rinse off. Remove skin from turkey and strip into bite size pieces. Boil in 10

KOREAN-STYLE BARBECUED TURKEY ROAST

2   pounds boneless turkey roast, sliced
2   cups soy sauce
1   cup sugar
1/3 cup sesame oil
1/2 teaspoon garlic powder
1   tablespoon sesame seeds (roasted)
1   tablespoon black pepper
3   green onions

Cut roots off of green onions and wash. Then mince. Mix all ingredients. Add sliced turkey and mix. Refrigerate for 1 day, turning over a couple times.

Put aluminum foil on top of barbecue grill, and then put turkey on. Barbecue. Serves 3-4 people.

BARBECUED BEEF RIBS

5   pounds beef ribs
2   green onions, minced
1/4 cup oyster sauce
1/4 cup worcestershire sauce
1/4 cup soy sauce
1/4 cup honey
1/2 teaspoon black pepper
1/2 teaspoon garlic, chopped
1   tablespoon sesame seeds (roasted)
1/2 teaspoon sesame oil
1/2 yellow onion, grated
1/8 cup sugar
1   tablespoon White Zinfandel Wine

Cut ribs in strips and wash well. In a large bowl mix remaining ingredients. Put ribs on a cookie sheet.

Bake: Brush some sauce on, and bake at 350 degrees for approximately 45 minutes. Brush on more sauce every 10 minutes. Turn over ribs half way through baking. Serve with rice. Serve 3-4 people.

BARBECUED SHORT RIBS

1   **pound beef short ribs (precut)**
2   **teaspoons sesame oil**
1/2 **cup soy sauce**
1/2 **cup water**
2   **teaspoons sesame seeds (roasted)**
3   **teaspoons sugar**
1   **teaspoon garlic powder**
1/2 **teaspoon pepper**

Wash ribs well. Make incisions in meat to help ribs marinate. Mix remaining ingredients together. Put ribs into the marinade. Allow ribs to marinate in sauce overnight in the refrigerator before cooking. Barbecue. Serve.

KOREAN-STYLE SPARE RIBS

2   **pounds spare ribs**
1/2 **cups soy sauce**
2   **green onions, 1-inch long**
2   **teaspoons garlic**
1/2 **cups sugar**
1/8 **cups sesame seeds (roasted)**
1   **tablespoon sesame oil**
1/8 **cup water**
1   **teaspoon black pepper**

Mix all ingredients except beef ribs together in a bowl. Add beef ribs. Mix together. Put into a closed container and refrigerate overnight. Barbecue. Serve with rice. Serves 2 people.

BAKED RIBS (KALBEE JHIM)

5   **pounds English cut beef ribs**
1   **cup soy sauce**
2   **cups carrots**
2   **cups daikon radish**
5   **green onions**
1   **tablespoon garlic powder**
2   **tablespoons sesame seeds (roasted)**
1   **tablespoon sugar (optional)**
1/2 **cup water**
1   **teaspoon black pepper**
1   **medium yellow onion**

Cut ribs into 2 inch pieces. Rinse and clean ribs well. Sprinkle sugar on each piece of meat. (Note: this helps with tenderization of the meat.)

Cut carrots into 1 inch pieces. Cut daikon into 1 inch pieces. Cut green onions into 1 inch pieces. Cut yellow onion into 2 inch pieces. Mix soy sauce, green onions, garlic powder, sesame seeds, sesame seed oil, black pepper, and water. Layer daikon and carrots on the bottom of the baking pan. Add meat on top of daikon and carrots. Then pour sauce over the meat, carrots and daikon.

Bake at 350 degrees for about 1 hour; make sure ribs are baked well. Serves 5-6 people.

BARBECUED NEW YORK-CUT STEAKS

5 New York-cut steaks
1 cup worcestershire sauce
1/2 cup honey
1/2 teaspoon black pepper
1/2 teaspoon crushed ginger
1 teaspoon chopped garlic
1 tablespoon grated yellow onion
1 tablespoon White Zinfandel Wine

Wash and clean steaks. Put in a pan. Mix remaining ingredients in a bowl. Brush sauce over steaks. Put in broiler and cook for 15 minutes each side, or until desired tenderness. Serve with rice. Serves 4-5 people.

HOT BARBECUED FILET MIGNON

6 filet mignon steaks
1 tablespoon White Zinfandel Wine
1/2 teaspoon chopped garlic
1/2 cup oyster sauce
1/2 cup soy sauce
1/2 cup honey
1/2 teaspoon black pepper
1 tablespoon hot paste
2 green onions, minced
1/2 yellow onion, grated

Wash steaks. Mix remaining ingredients in a bowl. Put steaks in a closed container. Pour sauce over steaks. Mix. Let sit in the refrigerator for 1 day, turning over once. Barbecue for 5 minutes each side, or until desired tenderness. Serve with rice. Serves 6 people.

KOREAN-STYLE BARBECUED STEAKS

2 pounds New York cut steaks
1/2 cup soy sauce
1/2 cup water
1/3 cup sugar
1/4 teaspoon black pepper
3 green onions, minced
1/4 teaspoon garlic powder

Mix all ingredients except steaks in a bowl. Wash steaks well. Use a paper towel to pat dry. Dunk steaks in sauce. Then put in a flat container. Pour remaining sauce over steaks.

Refrigerate for 1 day. Barbecue. Serve.

KIM'S GINGER FLAVORED BARBECUED STEAKS

2 teaspoons ginger, grated
2 pounds New York cut steaks
1/2 cup soy sauce
1/2 cup water
1/3 cup sugar
1/4 teaspoon black pepper
3 green onions, minced
1/4 teaspoon garlic powder

Mix all ingredients except steaks in a bowl. Wash steaks well. Use a paper towel to pat dry. Dunk steaks in sauce. Then put in a flat container. Pour remaining sauce over steaks.

Refrigerate for 1 day. Barbecue. Serve.

KOREAN-STYLE SHISHKEBABS

History: Most Korean people eat shishkebabs only for New Year's Day or for a death memorial.

1 bundle 12-inch long shishkebab sticks
2 pounds beef round
3 green onions, 6 inches long, without tops
3 asparagus, 6 inches long
1 tablespoon sesame seeds (roasted)
1 tablespoon soy sauce
1 tablespoon sesame oil
1 tablespoon sugar
1/4 teaspoon black pepper
1/2 teaspoon garlic powder

Mix all ingredients except meat. Cut meat in half, crosswise. Slice lengthwise to 6 inches long and 1/2-inch thick. Add to sauce. Mix. Cover in a bowl and refrigerate for one day.

Lay out 2 pieces of meat, one piece of green onion, 2 pieces of meat, and one piece of asparagus. Put one shishkebab stick through tops and bottoms of meat and vegetables. Barbecue. Put foil on top of grill first and then the meat sticks. Cook for 5 minutes each side. Check. Serve.

BROILED RIBEYE (BUIGOGI)

4 rib eye steaks
1 cup soy sauce
1 tablespoon garlic powder
4 tablespoons sugar
2 green onions, minced
1 tablespoon crushed sesame seeds (roasted)
1 teaspoon black pepper
2 tablespoons sesame oil

Combine soy sauce, garlic powder, sugar, green onions, sesame seeds, black pepper, and sesame seed oil. Allow steaks to marinate in sauce overnight in the refrigerator before cooking.

Broil or barbecue until done. Serve.

MIXED VEGETABLES WITH BEEF (CHOP CHEE)

(See color photograph.)

1   12 ounce package Dang Myun noodles
1   pound rib eye steak
10 dried mushrooms
2   bundles green onions
1   large yellow onion
2   bundles spinach
2   large carrots
3/4 teaspoon garlic salt (divided)
3   teaspoons sesame oil (divided)
1   tablespoon sesame seeds (roasted)
1/2 teaspoon black pepper
    Salt (optional to taste)
    Sugar (optional to taste)

Soak noodles for 1/2 hour. Bring to a boil 1 quart of water and cook noodles for 10 minutes. Rinse noodles in cold water and set aside.

Cut green onions into 2 inch long pieces. Cut carrots into 3 inch long slivers. Cut mushrooms into slivers. Cut the yellow onion in half and into strips. Cut roots off spinach and then cut the rest of the spinach in half.

Boil green onions in 1 quart of water for about a minute and rinse in cold water. Saute yellow onions on low heat for 2 minutes. Saute carrots with 1/4 teaspoon garlic salt and 1 teaspoon sesame seed oil on low heat for 5 minutes. Saute mushrooms with 1/4 teaspoon garlic salt and 1 teaspoon sesame seed oil on low heat for 10 minutes. Saute rib eye steak with 1/4 teaspoon garlic salt and 1 teaspoon sesame seed oil on low heat for 10 minutes.

Mix vegetables and noodles together. Add sesame seeds and black pepper. Sugar and salt (to taste). Serves 9-10 people.

SAUTÉED VEGETABLES WITH BEEF

1/2 pound portabella mushrooms, thinly sliced
1/2 pound bean sprouts
1   pound sirloin steak
3   cups leek
1   yellow onion
6   green onions, 1-inch long pieces
1/2 teaspoon chopped garlic
1   tablespoon sesame oil
1   tablespoon sesame seeds (roasted)
1   teaspoon hot pepper powder
1/4 teaspoon black pepper
1   teaspoon salt

Optional:
2   jalapeno peppers, without seeds, quartered

Wash mushrooms and then slice thin. Cut sirloin steaks like french fries. Saute meat in sesame oil for a few minutes. Cut leek into 1-inch long pieces. Quarter each leek. Cut yellow onion in half and slice each half into 1/4-inch thick slices. Add mushrooms and garlic. Saute for a few more minutes.

Cut bottoms off of green onions. Then cut into 1-inch long pieces. Quarter jalapeno peppers. Remove seeds. Add all ingredients to meat and saute another 5 minutes. Serves 3-4 people.

CHOP CHEE
(Mixed Vegetables with Beef)

BEEF AND MUSHROOM STIR FRY

1   package (about 32 ounces) oyster mushrooms
1   pound button mushrooms
5   green onions, 1-inch pieces
1   teaspoon crushed garlic
1   tablespoon sesame oil
1/2 teaspoon salt
1/2 teaspoon black pepper
1   pound cross rib steak (boneless)
1   medium yellow onion
1   tablespoon hot red bean paste

Slice onions, beef, and mushrooms. Fry beef for 5 minutes with 1 tablespoon sesame seed oil. In the same pan combine mushrooms, onions, garlic, pepper and salt with the beef. Stir fry for 5 more minutes. Serves 4-5 people.

KOREAN BEEF DUMPLINGS

2   cups flour
1   cup cold water
1/2 teaspoon salt
2   small potatoes, cubed
2   green onions, minced
1   teaspoon garlic powder
1   quart beef broth
1   quart water
2   tablespoons sesame seeds (roasted)

Boil 1 quart water. Add the potatoes and the soup stock. Boil for 10 minutes.

Mix flour and salt in a large bowl. Gradually add 1 cup cold water. Knead. It is done if, when you poke it, it doesn't bounce back. Split dough in half. Wet fingertips and then pull off bite-size piece and drop them into the soup.

Cook for 10 minutes, stirring occasionally. Taste to see when done. Turn off heat. Add green onions. Let sit for 5 minutes before serving. Serves 3-4 people.

KIM'S PORK AND BEEF MEATBALLS

1/2   **pound ground beef**
1/2   **pound ground pork**
2   **cups leek, minced**
1/2   **yellow onion, chopped**
2   **tablespoons sesame seeds (roasted)**
1   **teaspoon chopped garlic**
1   **tablespoon sesame oil**
1/2   **teaspoon black pepper**
1   **tablespoon hot pepper powder**
1/2   **teaspoon salt**
2   **eggs**

Heat 2 tablespoons sesame oil in a large pan. Mix all ingredients in a bowl. Make walnut-size balls and drop into pan. Fry over low heat, to golden brown. Leave in pan.

Sauce:

2   **cups water**
3   **beef bouillon cubes**
6   **green onions, minced**
1/2   **teaspoon sugar**
1   **tablespoon hot paste**

Heat 2 cups water. Add bouillon cubes and dissolve. Add remaining ingredients. Boil well for 10 minutes. When done pour over meatballs and boil for 5 more minutes. Serve with rice. Serves 4-5 people.

KOREAN MEAT PATTIES

1/2   **pound ground sirloin**
1/2   **pound ground pork**
2   **green onions, with tops**
1   **tablespoon sesame seeds (roasted)**
1   **teaspoon sesame oil**
1   **teaspoon soy sauce**
1/4   **teaspoon salt**
1/2   **teaspoon garlic powder**
1/8   **teaspoon black pepper (optional)**
   Vegetable oil
5   **eggs**

Finely mince green onions. In bowl, combine sirloin, pork, onions, sesame seeds, oil, soy sauce, salt, and garlic powder. If desired, add pepper. Mix well.

Form mixture into walnut-sized balls. Flatten to 1/2 inch thickness. Heat oil in lightly-oiled skillet. Place patties, in single layer, in the pan. Brown on one side, over medium heat. Turn. Flatten again with spatula and brown on second side. Set meat patties aside. Wash pan.

Heat small amount of vegetable oil in cleaned pan. Beat eggs slightly. Dip patties in egg and place, in single layer, in pan. Spoon 1 tablespoon of egg on each patty, and fry 3 minutes, over very low heat. Turn. Spoon 1 tablespoon of egg on each patty again. Fry another 3 minutes.

Meat patties are excellent with steamed short grain rice. Serves 6-8 people.

KIM'S BARBECUED MEAT PATTIES

2   pounds ground sirloin
2   tablespoons sesame oil
1   tablespoon sesame seeds (roasted)
1/2 teaspoon black pepper
1/2 teaspoon garlic, chopped
1   teaspoon sugar
1/2 teaspoon soy sauce
1/4 teaspoon salt
1   green onion, minced

Mix all ingredients in a bowl. Make hamburger size patties. Barbecue.

If you barbecue outside, put each patty in foil. Then cook. This keeps the meat patties moist. Serves 4-5 people.

BARBECUED PORK SPARERIBS

3   pounds pork spareribs
2   green onions, chopped
1/4 cup oyster sauce
1/4 cup worcestershire sauce
1/4 cup soy sauce
1/4 cup honey
1/2 teaspoon black pepper
1/2 teaspoon garlic, grated
1   tablespoon sesame seeds (roasted)
1/2 teaspoon sesame oil
1/2 yellow onion, grated
1/8 cup sugar

Cut spareribs in strips and wash well. In a large bowl mix remaining ingredients. Add spareribs and mix. Let sit for 1 day in the refrigerator, turning over once.

Barbecue or bake. If baked, cook at 350 degrees for 45 minutes. Brush on sauce while baking. Serve with rice. Serves 3-4 people.

SPICY BAKED RIBS

3   pounds pork ribs
4   tablespoons hot pepper paste
2   tablespoons sesame oil
2   tablespoons sesame seeds (roasted)
1   tablespoon crushed garlic
1   tablespoon sugar
5   green onions
1   tablespoon black pepper

Cut ribs into individual strips. Mince green onions. Combine all ingredients and mix well. Marinate ribs overnight in the refrigerator. Bake at 350 degrees for 15 minutes on each side. These ribs can be barbecued. Serves 3-4 people.

ROASTED PORK

1   5 pound boneless pork roast
1   tablespoon garlic salt
5   cups water

Sprinkle 1 tablespoon garlic salt over pork roast. In a large baking pan, place 5 cups of water and pork roast. Bake at 400 degrees for 60 minutes. Reduce heat to 350 degrees and bake for 4 1/2 hours. Let cool for 30 minutes and then slice and serve with Kim Chee and rice. Serves 5-6 people.

KIM'S SPECIAL FRIED PORK LOIN

6   boneless pork loins
3   cups cabbage, shredded
1   English cucumber, sliced
1   cup bread crumbs
3   eggs
2   cups olive oil

Optional:
    oyster sauce

Wash pork loins. Dab water off. Beat 3 eggs in a bowl. Dip pork loins in eggs, then in bread crumbs, coating well. Heat 2 cups olive oil in frying pan. Fry pork loins, approximately 10 minutes each side, or until golden brown.

Shred cabbage and put 1 cup on each plate. Put pork loins on plate. Place cucumbers on plate too. Top with oyster sauce. Serves 3-4 people.

BARBECUED PORK LOINS

1 1/2   pound boneless center cut pork loin
1   green onion, minced
1   teaspoon black pepper
1   teaspoon garlic salt
1   teaspoon sugar (optional)
2   teaspoons sesame seeds (roasted)
1   teaspoon hot paste
2   teaspoons sesame oil
4   teaspoons soy sauce

Slice pork into paper thin slices. Wash pork in cold water. Mix remaining ingredients together. Marinate pork for about an hour in the refrigerator. Barbecue until well done. Serves 2-3 people.

KIM'S SWEET AND SOUR PORK (KOREAN STYLE)

1 cup pineapple slices (optional)
1 pound boneless pork loin
1 English cucumber
2 medium carrots
3 green onions
1 small yellow onion

Batter:

1/4 teaspoon salt
1 cup water
1 cup cornstarch
1/2 cup flour

Sauce:

3 tablespoons rice vinegar
4 tablespoons sugar (or more to taste)
3 cups water

Batter: Mix salt, 1 cup water, 1 cup cornstarch and 1/2 cup flour until there are no lumps.

Cut pork into 3 inch strips and dip into batter. Deep fry for 6 minutes.

Slice yellow and green onions into 2 inch pieces. Slice cucumbers and carrots into very thin pieces. Set aside vegetables.

Mix 1/2 cup cornstarch with 1 cup of water and set aside.

Put remaining 2 cups of water in a saucepan and bring to a boil. Add slowly corn starch and water mixture. Stir and continue boiling for 5 minutes. Add onions, carrots, cucumbers and pineapple slices. Stir and pour over pork. Serves 5-6 people.

HOT BARBECUED PORK LOIN

1 tablespoon White Zinfandel Wine
6 pork loins
1/2 teaspoon chopped garlic
1/2 cup oyster sauce
1/2 cup soy sauce
1/2 cup honey
1/2 teaspoon black pepper
1 tablespoon hot paste
2 green onions, chopped
1/2 yellow onion, grated

Wash pork loin. Sprinkle lightly with salt. Mix remaining ingredients in a bowl. Put loin in pan and pour sauce on top. Bake at 350 degrees for 45 minutes. Check periodically. Serve with rice. Serves 3 people.

HOT BARBECUED PORK CHOPS

1 tablespoon White Zinfandel Wine
1/2 teaspoon garlic, grated
1/2 cup oyster sauce
1/2 cup soy sauce
1/2 cup honey
1/2 teaspoon black pepper
1 tablespoon hot paste
2 green onions, minced
1/2 yellow onion, grated
6 pork chops

Wash pork chops. Mix remaining ingredients in a bowl. Put pork chops in pan and pour sauce on top.

Bake at 350 degrees for 45 minutes. Check periodically. Serve with rice. Serves 3 people.

BAKED LAMB SHANKS

3-4 lamb shoulders
2 lamb shanks
1/2 cup soy sauce
2 green onions, 1-inch long pieces
2 teaspoons garlic powder
1/2 cup sugar
1/8 cup sesame seeds (roasted)
1 tablespoon black pepper

Wash meat well. Put lamb shanks and shoulder on a cookie sheet. Cut bottoms off of green onions and wash. Cut into 1-inch long pieces. Mix remaining ingredients in a bowl. Brush some sauce on lamb meat.

Heat oven to 350 degrees. Cook lamb for approximately 45 minutes, brushing on more sauce every 5 minutes. Serves 2-3 people.

BAKED LAMB CHOPS

6 lamb chops
1/2 cup soy sauce
2 green onions, 1-inch long pieces
2 teaspoons garlic powder
1/2 cup sugar
1/8 cup sesame seeds (roasted)
1 tablespoon black pepper

Wash lamb chops well. Put lamb chops on a cookie sheet. Cut bottoms off of green onions and wash. Cut into 1-inch long pieces. Mix remaining ingredients in a bowl. Brush some sauce on lamb chops. Heat oven to 350 degrees. Cook lamb for approximately 1/2 hour, brushing on more sauce every 5 minutes. Serves 3-4 people.

HOT BAKED RAINBOW TROUT

1-2 pounds rainbow trout
2   cups soy sauce
1   tablespoon hot paste
1   tablespoon hot pepper powder
2   green jalapeno peppers, chopped, seedless
1   tablespoon sesame seeds (roasted)
1/2 teaspoon chopped garlic
1   teaspoon sesame oil
1/4 teaspoon black pepper
1/2 teaspoon sugar
3   green onions, chopped
    olive oil

Scale and wash fish well. Dab dry with a towel. Mix all ingredients except rainbow trout in a bowl. Put trout in a pan. Brush olive oil over top and bottom of fish.

Bake at 350 degrees for approximately 30 minutes, or to a golden brown. Pour sauce over fish and bake for approximately another 10 minutes. Serve with rice. Serves 2-3 people.

BAKED MACKEREL

1   pound whole mackerel
2   green onions (chopped)
1   tablespoon crushed garlic
1/4 cup hot pepper powder
1   tablespoon sesame oil
1   tablespoon sesame seeds (roasted)
1/2 teaspoon sugar
1   cup soy sauce

Slice mackerel from head to tail on it's stomach side. Scale and clean fish. Combine green onions, garlic, hot pepper powder, sesame seed oil, sesame seeds, soy sauce and sugar. Stuff fish with the soy sauce combination. Bake for 10 minutes on each side or longer if desired. Serves 3-5 people.

BAKED LING COD

1   pound Ling cod fish fillets
1   cup soy sauce
1   tablespoon sesame oil
1   teaspoon hot pepper powder
2   green onions, chopped
1   teaspoon garlic powder
1   teaspoon sugar

Combine soy sauce, sesame seeds, sesame seed oil, hot pepper powder, onions, garlic powder, and sugar. Pour sauce over fish and bake for 30 minutes at 350 degrees. Serves 3-5 people.

BAKED RAINBOW TROUT

3   pounds fresh rainbow trout
1   jalapeno pepper
3   green onions, with tops
2   cloves garlic
1   cup soy sauce
1/2 teaspoon sesame oil
1   teaspoon sesame seeds (roasted)
1   teaspoon hot red pepper powder

Wash fish; remove scales and the head if you desire. In each fish, cut 4-5 diagonal slits to the bone. Line low sided cookie sheet with aluminum foil. Place whole fish in single layers in pan and bake at 550 degrees until golden brown, approximately 20 minutes.

While fish is cooking, make sauce: Cut pepper in lengthwise quarters and remove seeds. Chop pepper and onions into small pieces. Finely mince garlic. In small bowl combine pepper, onion, garlic, and next 4 ingredients. Spoon sauce over browned fish. Turn oven temperature to 400 degrees and continue to bake for 10 minutes.

Serve baked fish with chighe, rice, and cucumber salad. Serves 3-5 people.

BAKED TROUT WITH HOT SAUCE

1   12-inch long trout (with head)
2 1/2 cups soy sauce
2   tablespoons hot pepper powder
1/2 teaspoon chopped garlic
3   green onions, chopped
5   jalapeno peppers, chopped, seedless
1   tablespoon hot sauce
1   tablespoon sesame seeds (roasted)
1   tablespoon sesame oil
    olive oil

Scale and clean trout. In a large 3-inch deep pan, spread oil over bottom so fish will not stick. Place fish in pan. Bake in oven at 350 degrees, for approximately 20 minutes, or until golden brown. Mix remaining ingredients in a bowl and pour over fish. Bake another 15 minutes. Serve with rice. Serves 3-4 people.

FRIED FLOUNDER

1/2 pound flounder, fillet
     salt
     flour (for coating fish)
  3 eggs (optional)

Batter:
  1 cup flour
  1 cup water
     Olive or vegetable oil for frying

Cut each piece of filleted fish in thirds. Spread fish in single layers on a platter and sprinkle lightly with salt. After 10 minutes, rinse with cold water; drain,* and coat fish with flour. (Optional: dip floured fish into lightly-beaten eggs). Prepare batter by combining flour and water. Dip fish into batter. Heat enough oil to just cover bottom of frying pan. Fry fish at medium temperature until golden brown, approximately 2 minutes on each side. Serve 5-6 people.

* Completely dry fish by spreading on paper towels and patting with additional towels.

FRIED KING FISH

    3 pounds King fish fillets
1 1/8 cups water
    1 cup flour
  1/4 teaspoon salt
    1 tablespoon oil
       Vegetable oil for frying

Slice fish into 2-inch long pieces. Lay on platter and sprinkle lightly with salt. Let sit in refrigerator for 1/2 hour. Wash well. Mix the batter and stir the fish into it. Heat a pan, put oil in and then fry the fish. Cook each side for approximately 5 minutes. Serves 2-4 people.

HOT BAKED PERCH TROUT

1-2 pounds perch trout
1/2 cup soy sauce
  1 tablespoon sesame seeds (roasted)
1/2 teaspoon chopped garlic
  1 teaspoon sesame oil
1/4 teaspoon black pepper
  1 tablespoon hot pepper powder
1/2 teaspoon sugar
  3 green onions, chopped
     olive oil

Scale and wash fish well. Dab dry with a towel. Mix all ingredients except perch trout in a bowl. Put trout in a pan. Brush olive oil over top and bottom of fish. Bake at 350 degrees for approximately 30 minutes, or to a golden brown. Pour sauce over fish and bake for approximately another 10 minutes. Serve with rice. Serves 2-3 people.

FISH AND CHIPS

1   pound smelt fillets
1   medium potato
1 1/2   cups flour
1 1/2   cups cornstarch
1 1/2   cups water
1   teaspoon salt
2   cups vegetable oil

Mix flour, cornstarch, water and salt in a bowl. Set aside. Heat 2 cups oil in a frying pan. Test with a small piece of onion; if bubbles come up and it sizzles, the oil is hot enough. Cut potato into rounds 1/4 inch thick. Dip in batter and fry to a golden brown. Put 1 cup flour on a plate and then put fish on plate. Dab fish in flour. Then dip smelts in the batter and fry to a golden brown. Serves 2-3 people.

Can serve with half portion vinegar and half portion soy sauce mixed. Dunk fish chips in sauce to eat.

BARBECUED SALMON STEAKS

4   salmon steaks
1   tablespoon White Zinfandel Wine
1   tablespoon sesame seeds (roasted)
1   tablespoon sesame oil
2   tablespoons soy sauce
2   tablespoons worcestershire sauce
2   tablespoons oyster sauce
1/2   teaspoon garlic powder
1/2   teaspoon black pepper
1/2   cup honey
3   green onions, chopped
1   tablespoon sugar

Mix all ingredients except salmon in a bowl. Set aside. Wash and clean fish. Dab dry. Brush oil on broiler grill. Put fish down. Brush sauce on top and cook for approximately 5 minutes. Turn over and put more sauce on other side, and cook for approximately 5 more minutes. Serves 4 people.

STEAMED SALMON

2 1/2   pounds salmon
1/3   cup salt
    olive oil

Wash fish. Dab dry with a towel. Slice through the middle, but not all the way through. Sprinkle salt inside fish and on top and bottom. Let sit in the refrigerator for 1 day. Wash off salmon. Rub olive oil on top and bottom of fish.

Steam for approximately 1/2 hour. Serves 3-4 people.

BAKED SALMON

2 1/2   pounds salmon
1/4   cup salt
      olive oil

Wash salmon well. Dab dry with a towel. Slice in the middle but not all the way through. Sprinkle salt inside fish, on top and on bottom. Let sit for approximately 1 hour. Wash off. Rub olive oil over top and bottom of fish. Bake in oven at 300 degrees for approximately 45 minutes, or until golden brown. Serve with rice. Serves 3-4 people.

BAKED SALMON STEAKS

2 1/2   pounds salmon steaks, 1 inch thick
2   cups soy sauce
1   cup sugar
1/3   cup sesame oil
1/2   teaspoon garlic powder
1   tablespoon sesame seeds (roasted)
1   tablespoon black pepper
3   green onions, chopped
      olive oil

Wash salmon. Dab dry with a towel. Set aside. Wash off green onions and cut off roots. Chop. Mix all ingredients except fish in a bowl. Rub olive oil on steaks and put in a pan. Bake for about 10 minutes at 350 degrees, until golden brown. Brush some sauce on steaks. Cook for approximately 1/2 hour, brushing on more sauce every 10 minutes. Serves 5 people.

HOT BAKED SALMON

2 1/2   pounds salmon
3   cup soy sauce
1/2   cup White Zinfandel wine
1/8   cup sesame oil
1/4   cup hot pepper powder
1/8   cup sugar
1/4   cup sesame seeds (roasted)
1/2   teaspoon garlic, chopped
1/4   teaspoon black pepper
3   green onions, chopped
3   jalapeno peppers, without seeds, quartered
      olive oil

Wash salmon well. Dab dry with a towel. Rub olive oil on top and bottom of fish. Cook in oven at 350 degrees for approximately 10 minutes, or until golden brown.

Wash green onions and cut off roots. Chop. Quarter jalapeno peppers and remove seeds. Mix all ingredients except fish in a bowl. When fish is done, pour sauce over and cook for another 20 minutes approximately, or until golden brown. While baking, scoop up sauce from around fish and pour over again. Serves 2-3 people.

KOREAN BARBECUED SALMON STEAKS

2 1/2   pounds salmon steaks, 1-inch thick
2   cups soy sauce
1   cup sugar
1/3   cup sesame oil
1/2   teaspoon garlic powder
1   tablespoon sesame seeds (roasted)
1   tablespoon black pepper
3   green onions, chopped
1/2   cup White Zinfandel wine
    olive oil

Clean and wash salmon. Dab dry with a towel. Set aside. Cut bottoms off of green onions and wash. Then chop. Mix all ingredients except salmon in a flat container. Brush some sauce on top and bottom of salmon. Barbecue on top of aluminum foil. Serves 3-4 people.

FRIED MUSHROOMS WITH SHRIMP

1/2   pound portabella mushrooms
1/2   pound bean sprouts
1/2   pound button mushrooms, thinly sliced
1   pound black tiger prawns (long or small)
3   cups leeks, 1-inch long pieces, quartered
1   yellow onion
6   green onions, 1-inch long pieces
1/2   teaspoon chopped garlic
3   tablespoons sesame oil
1   tablespoon sesame seeds (roasted)
1   teaspoon hot pepper powder
1/4   teaspoon black pepper
1   teaspoon salt

Optional:
2   jalapeno peppers, without seeds, quartered

Wash mushrooms and slice thin. Set aside. Cut bottoms off of green onions and wash. Then cut into 1-inch long pieces. Cut yellow onion in half and slice each half into 1/4-inch thick slices. Cut jalapeno peppers, if desired.

Saute bean sprouts, leek, yellow onion, green onions, and jalapeno peppers if desired, in 1 tablespoon sesame oil. Cook for 5 minutes. Set aside on a plate.

Saute mushrooms, garlic, and salt in 1 tablespoon sesame oil for a few minutes. Set aside on a plate.

Take shells off prawns and wash. Drain and then saute in 1 tablespoon sesame oil for a few minutes. Add mushrooms, vegetables and remaining seasonings, and saute for a few more minutes. Serve with rice. Serves 2-3 people.

KOREAN ANCHOVY DUMPLINGS

Dumplings:

2 cups flour
1 cup cold water
1/2 teaspoon salt

Anchovy Soup Stock:

2 potatoes, small cubes
2 green onions, chopped
1 teaspoon garlic powder
2 tablespoons anchovy soup mix
1 quart water
2 tablespoons sesame seeds (roasted)

Boil 1 quart water. Add the potatoes and soup stock. Boil for 10 minutes. Mix flour and salt in large bowl. Gradually add 1 cup cold water. Knead. It is not done if it bounces back when you poke it. Split dough in half. Wet fingertips. Pull off bite-size pieces and drop them into the soup.

Cook for 10 minutes. Stir occasionally. Turn off heat. Put in green onions. Let sit for 5 minutes before serving. Serves 2-3 people.

POTATO DUMPLINGS WITH BEEF SOUP STOCK

Dumplings:

2 cups flour
1 cup cold water
1/2 teaspoon salt

Soup stock:

3 green onions, chopped
2 zucchinis, cut in half and sliced
1 cup grated potatoes
1 quart beef stock
1 teaspoon garlic powder

Optional:

Hot pepper powder

Peel potatoes and grate. Put in a bowl. Add 1 1/2 cups flour and cold water. Knead for 20 minutes. Gradually add the remaining 1/2 cup of flour. It is done if, when you poke it, it doesn't bounce back out. Set aside.

Bring soup stock to a boil. Get a small bowl with water in it and moisten fingertips. Tear dough into bite-size pieces and drop into soup. Cook. Done when dumplings rise to the top.

Add garlic, salt, zucchini and onions. Cook for 5 minutes. Turn off heat and let sit for another 5 minutes. Add salt to taste. Serves 2-3 people.

POTATO DUMPLINGS WITH CLAM FLAVOR

1   cup grated potatoes
2   cups flour
3   green onions, chopped
2   zucchinis
7   cups water, divided
1/2 cup clam soup mix
1   teaspoon garlic
1   teaspoon salt

Optional:

hot pepper powder

Peel potatoes and then grate. Put in a bowl. Add 1 1/2 cups flour and 1 cup water. Knead for 20 minutes. Gradually add the remaining 1/2 cup flour. It is done if, when you poke it, it doesn't bounce back out. Set aside.

Boil 6 cups water. Add clam soup mix. Bring to a boil. Get a small bowl with water in it and moisten fingertips. Tear dough into bite-size pieces and drop into soup. Cook. Done when dumplings rise to top.

Cut zucchini in half and slice. Add garlic, salt, zucchini and onions to soup. Cook for 5 minutes. Add salt to taste. Serves 2-3 people.

VEGETARIAN FRIED MUSHROOMS

1/2 pound portabella mushrooms, thinly sliced
1/2 pound bean sprouts
1/2 pound button mushrooms, thinly sliced
3   cups leek
1   yellow onion
6   green onions, 1-inch long pieces
1/2 teaspoon chopped garlic
2   tablespoons sesame oil
1   tablespoon sesame seeds (roasted)
1   teaspoon hot pepper powder
1/4 teaspoon black pepper
1   teaspoon salt

Optional:

2   jalapeno peppers, without seeds, quartered

Wash mushrooms and then slice thin. Saute mushrooms, garlic and salt in 1 tablespoon sesame oil for a few minutes. Set aside on a plate.

Cut bottoms off of green onions and wash. Then cut into 1-inch long pieces. Cut leek into 1-inch long pieces also. Quarter each round. Cut yellow onion in half and slice each half into 1/4-inch thick slices. Cut jalapeno peppers, if desired.

Saute bean sprouts, leek, yellow onion, green onions and jalapeno peppers if desired, in 1 tablespoon sesame soil. Saute for 5 minutes.

Add mushrooms and remaining seasonings to vegetables. Cook for a few more minutes and serve. Serve with rice. Serves 2-3 people.

SUE'S SPECIAL VEGETARIAN DISH

1/2	pound portabella mushrooms, sliced
3	jalapeno peppers, quartered, seedless
1	yellow onion, sliced
1	bell pepper, sliced
7	cups celery, sliced
1/2	pound pea pods
1/2	pound bean sprouts
3	cups cabbage, sliced
2	medium tomatoes, quartered
5	green onions, cut into 2-inch long pieces
1/2	cup flour or cornstarch
1	tablespoon salt
1/2	teaspoon garlic powder
1	tablespoon hot paste
1/2	teaspoon black pepper

Optional:

6	chicken or beef bouillon cubes

Cut yellow onion and bell pepper in half and slice. Slice mushrooms. Quarter tomatoes and jalapeno peppers. Cut celery slightly diagonally into approximately 1-inch long sections. Cut cabbage in half and then slice into 1/2-inch thick slices.

Boil 6 cups water and add mushrooms. Let cook for a few seconds, take out and rinse with cold water. Wash peas and set aside. Put bean sprouts in 6 cups water and boil for a few seconds. Take out, rinse with cold water and set aside. Boil 6 cups water again and add yellow onion, green onions, bell pepper, celery, pea pods, jalapeno peppers and cabbage. Boil for a few seconds, take out and rinse. Set aside.

Boil 3 new cups of water. Add bouillon cubes, if using. When dissolved, remove 1 cup and put in a bowl, but keep remaining 2 cups water boiling. Mix the 1 cup water with flour or cornstarch. Add mixture slowly to

the 2 cups boiling water and stir. Add black pepper, hot paste, garlic powder and salt. Cook for 5 minutes on low heat.

Add cooked vegetables to sauce. Mix and serve with rice. Serves 4-5 people.

FLOUR NOODLES WITH SPINACH

1/4 teaspoon garlic salt
1 teaspoon hot pepper powder
3 ounces Somen Japanese Noodles
1/4 teaspoon sesame oil
1/4 cup dried clam soup mix
1 tablespoon sesame seeds (roasted)
3 cups water
1 teaspoon soy sauce
2 bundles spinach, chopped
2 green onions
1/4 teaspoon sugar

Boil 5 cups water, and add noodles and cook for 5 minutes. Then rinse noodles with cold water and drain. Set aside.

Boil 3 cups water and add 1/4 cup dried clam soup mix. Boil for 10 minutes. Set aside.

Cut off roots of spinach and wash. Boil 1 quart water and stir in spinach. Cook for 5 minutes. When done, rinse with cold water.

Chop green onions and mix with spinach. Add 1 tablespoon sesame seeds, 1/4 teaspoon sesame oil, 1 teaspoon garlic salt, 1/4 teaspoon black pepper, 1 teaspoon soy sauce and 1/4 teaspoon sugar. Mix together.

When ready to eat, put noodles in a dish and pour clam stock over noodles. Put spinach on top of clam stock. Serves 2-3 people.

BLACK SAUCE NOODLES (JA JUNG)

5 potatoes
1 pound boneless pork loin chops
2 medium yellow onions
5 green onions
1 teaspoon garlic powder
1/4 teaspoon black pepper
1/2 cup cornstarch
1 teaspoon sugar
1 cup cold water
4 cups water
1/4 cup "Orchids" Chinese style black soy bean paste
14 ounces "Azumaya" Japanese style noodles

Peel potatoes. Cut into 1/3 to 1/2 inch cubes. Bring to boil 2 quarts of water. Add potatoes. Stirring occasionally, cook until almost done. (Potatoes will be crunchy). Rinse in cold water. Set aside.

Chop pork and yellow onions in same size cubes as potatoes. Cut green onions in 1/2 inch pieces. Fry pork and garlic in 1 tablespoon vegetable oil for 10 minutes, stirring constantly. Add yellow and green onions, and cook for another 5 minutes. Add pepper. Set aside.

For gravy, combine cornstarch and sugar. Gradually blend into 1 cup cold water, stirring until smooth.

Bring 4 cups water to boil. Add bean paste. Turn heat down to medium. Stirring constantly, slowly add cornstarch mixture. Cook and stir for 5 minutes. Add potatoes and pork mixture; continue to cook for an additional 5 minutes.

Cook noodles in 2 quarts boiling water until done, about 10 minutes. Drain and rinse in cold water.

Put individual serving of noodles on plate. Spoon sauce over noodles. Serves 4-5 people.

KOREAN-STYLE NOODLES,
WITH SEASONED ZUCCHINI

(This dish is especially good when topped also with Spinach Salad).

1   pound dried Korean noodles (wheat)
1/4 cup clam dashida soup stock OR
1/4 cup anchovy soup stock
2   zucchini
1   stalk green onion, minced
1/4 teaspoon sesame oil
1   teaspoon soy sauce
1   teaspoon sesame seeds (roasted)
1/2 teaspoon garlic powder, divided

Zucchini: Bring 5 cups water to boil. Add zucchini, and stir.

Cook for 5 minutes. Drain and rinse with cold water. Squeeze out as much water as possible. Add onion, sesame oil, soy sauce, sesame seeds, and 1/8 teaspoon garlic powder. Stir, and set aside.

Bring 8 cups of water to a boil. Cook noodles, stirring occasionally, until done about 10 minutes. Rinse in cold water and drain. Set aside. Bring 8 cups of water to a boil. Add clam dashida or anchovy stock and garlic powder. Stir and boil 5 minutes.

Place noodles in individual bowls. Top with seasoned zucchini. Serves 4-5 people.

RAMEN (WU DUNG)

14   ounces Japanese-style noodles
2   ounces Ono Kamaboko (steamed fish cakes,
     approximately 1/3 of 5.64 ounce package)
2   ounces "Azumaya" Tempura deep fried fish cakes
     (approximately 1/3 of 6 ounce package)
2   green onions, with tops
1/4 cup anchovy soup stock
1/8 teaspoon garlic powder, or to taste (optional)
1-2 eggs (optional)

Cook noodles in 2 quarts boiling water for about 5 minutes. (Noodles will be chewy but not completely done). Drain and rinse in cold water. Set aside.

Cut steamed and deep fried fish cakes in 1/3 inch slices. Chop onions. Set aside.

Bring to boil 1 quart water. Add soup stock, noodles, fish cakes, onions, and, if you wish, garlic powder. Continue boiling for about 10 minutes, or until noodles are done.

Optional: Vigorously stir well-beaten eggs into mixture just before removing from heat. Serves 4-5 people.

LETTUCE WITH RICE (SUM)

1 head red lettuce or leaf lettuce
2 tablespoons soybean paste
1 tablespoon hot paste
1 teaspoon sesame oil
2 teaspoons sesame seeds (roasted)
1/2 teaspoon chopped garlic
3 jalapeno peppers, without seeds, minced
3 green onions, minced
1/2 teaspoon sugar

Cut top off lettuce and wash. Drain.

Mix remaining ingredients in a bowl. Put desired amount of cooked rice in one lettuce leaf. Top with desired amount of sauce. Roll up. Ready to serve. Serves 3-5 people.

SPINACH WITH RICE

1 bundle of spinach
2 tablespoons soybean paste
1 tablespoon hot paste
1 teaspoon sesame oil
2 teaspoons sesame seeds (roasted)
1/2 teaspoon chopped garlic
3 jalapeno peppers, without seeds, minced
3 green onions, minced
1/2 teaspoon sugar

Cut top off spinach and wash. Drain. Put desired amount of cooked rice in a spinach leaf. Add desired amount of sauce. Roll up. Ready to serve. Serves 3-5 people.

COLD NOODLE DISH (NENGMYEON BROTH)

3 quarts water
1 chicken
2 pounds beef bone
1/2 medium cabbage
1 yellow onion
3 pieces of garlic
1 green onion
2 quarts water
1 English cucumber
3 eggs
1 Asian pear
26 ounces Oriental Style Noodles

Peel skin off chicken. Cook chicken and beef bone in 8 cups water, for 10 minutes. Throw water away. Wash chicken and bone well. Put 3 quarts water in a pot. Add chicken and beef bone. Cut off top and root of green onion. Peel the skin off of garlic. Put garlic, green onion, 1/2 cabbage and 1/2 yellow onion with chicken. Cook for 1 hour.

Remove meat and vegetables, and throw away. Strain broth through a cheesecloth. Place broth in plastic container. Put in refrigerator for about an hour, to make cold.

Hard boil the eggs in their shells. Peel and cut in half when done. Slice cucumber like thin french fries. Peel Asian pear and slice thin. Boil 2 quarts water. Add noodles and cook for 10 minutes.

Rinse with cold water. Put in a bowl. Put cucumbers in the noodles, then the Asian pear, and then the hard boiled eggs. Top with cold broth. You may add soy sauce or vinegar for more flavor. Serves 5-6 people.

STEAMED SWEET RICE WITH RED BEANS AND CHESTNUTS

5   **cups sweet rice**
2   **cups chestnuts (precooked)**
1/2   **cup red beans (oriental and dried)**
5+12 **cups water (divided)**
1/2   **teaspoon salt**

Wash rice well. Soak in water for 1 hour. Wash and cook beans in 5 cups of water for a half hour on low. Wash rice again until water turns clear. Strain rice and mix chestnuts, beans and salt.

Add 12 cups of water to a steamer and place the mixture in a cheesecloth and steam for about 45 minutes. Serves 5-6 people.

STEAMED CABBAGE WITH RICE

1   **head of cabbage**
2   **tablespoons soybean paste**
1   **tablespoon hot paste**
1   **teaspoon sesame oil**
2   **teaspoons sesame seeds (roasted)**
1/2   **teaspoon chopped garlic**
3   **jalapeno peppers, without seeds, minced**
3   **green onions, minced**
1/2   **teaspoon sugar**

Split cabbage in half and steam or boil it. If you boil it, put in 5 cups of water, and cook for 10 minutes, or until desired tenderness. Strain.

Mix remaining ingredients. Put desired amount of cooked rice in a cabbage leaf. Top with desired amount of sauce. Roll up. Ready to serve. Serves 3-5 people.

NAPA CABBAGE WITH RICE

1   **head of Napa cabbage or red lettuce**
2   **tablespoons soybean paste**
1   **tablespoon hot sauce paste**
1   **teaspoon sesame oil**
2   **teaspoons sesame seeds (roasted)**
1/2   **teaspoon chopped cabbage**
3   **jalapeno peppers, without seeds, minced**
3   **green onions, minced**
1/2   **teaspoon sugar**

Cut top off cabbage and wash. Drain. Mix remaining ingredients in a bowl. Put desired amount of cooked rice in a cabbage leaf. Add desired amount of sauce. Roll up. Ready to serve. Serves 3-5 people.

Notes

Desserts

MOHCHEE
(SWEET RICE CAKES WITH FILLING)

5	lbs. sweet rice flour
18	oz. sweet red bean paste
3/4	teaspoon salt
10	cups water

Pour three quarts of water into the bottom of the steamer pan. Combine sweet rice flour, salt and water. Mix thoroughly until there are no lumps. Saturate cheese cloth evenly in the steamer. Pour 1/3 of the mixture over the cheese cloth and cover pan. Steam for 30 minutes on high heat.

(Tip: Mohchee is completely cooked when it does not stick to the cheese cloth when pulled back.)

Let stand for five minutes before removing from pan. Place Mohchee on corn starch coated cookie sheet. Break off 2 tablespoon portions and form a cup from the Mohchee ball, using the dry side as the inside, don't pull too thin. Fill with 1 tablespoon of red bean paste. Pull up sides, one at a time, making sure there are no holes in the Mohchee dough. Give the top a twist and smooth into a round ball. Then press to flatten to a 1/2 inch in height. Dust lightly with cornstarch to prevent sticking. Serve.

Can only be stored in the refrigerator up to 3 days, before expiring.

SWEET RICE CAKES

4	cups dried red beans (Oriental)
1-1/8	teaspoon salt, divided
2	pounds sweet rice flour
1	cup water

Wash beans and put in a large, heavy pot in 1 quart of water. Cover, and boil rapidly for 1 hour. Turn heat down; simmer for additional hour, or until beans are just moist and most of the water is gone. (Check occasionally during cooking to be sure pot is not dry). Cool for 1/2 hour. Mix in 1/8 teaspoon salt. Pound with pestle and mortar until 1/2 of beans are crushed and look fluffy. Set aside.

Put rice flour into a large bowl. Gradually blend in 1 cup of water by sprinkling a little at a time over flour, mixing well with hands after each addition. (Small amount of moistened flour will form lumps when squeezed). Sift flour, and stir in 1 teaspoon of salt.

Put 1 quart of water in a large steamer bottom. Cover holes in food holder with cheese cloth. Put 1/2 beans in steamer, add rice flour, and top with remaining beans. Steam over rapidly boiling water for 45 minutes. Ready to Serve.

SWEET BEAN DUMPLINGS

16   ounces sweet rice flour
1/8 teaspoon salt
1   cup warm water
1   can (16 ounces) sweetened red bean paste
     Sugar (optional)

Mix rice flour and salt in bowl. Gradually blend in 1 cup of water. Knead dough for about 20 minutes. Cover with plastic wrap or aluminum foil. Set aside for approximately 1/2 hour.

Bring 5 cups of water to boil. Stir in bean paste and, if you wish, sugar to taste. Knead dough second time for 10 minutes. Form 1 inch balls. Drop balls gently into boiling bean-paste sauce.

Dumplings will rise to surface when cooked, in about 5 minutes. Serves 5-6 People.

STEAMED SWEET RICE WITH DATES AND CHESTNUTS

14   ounces dried red dates
12   ounces dried chestnuts
5   cups sweet rice
1/2 cup dark brown sugar, or to taste
1   teaspoon soy sauce
1   teaspoon sesame oil
     Pine nuts

Wash dates well and soak for a 1/2 hour. (To retain proper texture, do not over soak). Remove stems and discard. Cut out pits–some meat will cling to pits. Put pits into a small pan with a 1/2 cup of water. Boil slowly for 10 minutes. Cool. With fingers remove remaining meat and add to juice from boiled pits. Discard pits, and set aside juice.

Soak chestnuts overnight. Wash well and drain. Boil at a high temperature for 10 minutes in 1 quart of water. Rinse and drain. Set aside.

Wash rice and soak in enough water to cover for 3 hours. Rinse well and drain in sieve. Put 1 quart of water in the bottom of a large steamer. If holes in food holder tray are large, cover with cheese cloth to prevent rice from falling through. Steam over rapidly boiling water for a 1/2 hour. Cool.

Put rice in a large bowl. Mixing well after each addition, blend in sugar, date juice, soy sauce, sesame oil, and whole dates and chestnuts. Spoon mixture into steamer, and cook over rapidly boiling water for 10 minutes.

Place layer of rice mixture in serving bowl or platter. Sprinkle 2 tablespoons (or as desired) pine nuts on rice. Continue alternating rice and nuts in 5-6 layers, ending with nuts. Serve.

STEAMED CORNBREAD WITH RED BEANS

History: About 50 years ago, during the Korean War, Korea received aid from America. Among other supplies, they sent over some corn meal. My mother didn't know what to do with it at first and then she made up this recipe. She died and I was not able to get this recipe from her. I remembered the taste and tried to recreate the cornbread. It turned out just like when my mother made it, when I was a child.

1	cup flour
2	cups corn meal
1/2	teaspoon baking powder
1/2	teaspoon baking soda
1/4	teaspoon salt
14	cups water (divided)
1/8	cup sugar
1/2	cup dried red beans (Oriental)

Wash and cook red beans in 6 cups water, for approximately 1/2 hour. Check. There should not be any water left in the pan. Cook well, and set aside.

Mix remaining ingredients in a bowl. Set aside for 1/2 hour.

Put 8 cups water in a large steamer. Spread a damp cheesecloth over it, leaving the corners hanging out. Pour in batter and sprinkle beans over the batter. Push beans in lightly with a spoon. Cover steamer with lid, and steam for 45 minutes. Turn heat off and let sit for 5 minutes. Lift up a corner of the cheesecloth. If cornbread comes off then it is done. Take out and serve.

STEAMED CORNBREAD WITH PINTO BEANS

5	cups flour
2 1/2	cups cornmeal
1	teaspoon baking soda
1	teaspoon baking powder
1	teaspoon salt
1	cup sugar
14	cups water (divided)
1-2	cups pinto beans

Wash and cook beans in 6 cups water for approximately 1/2 hour. Check. There should not be any water left in the pan. Put aside.

Mix remaining ingredients in a bowl. Set aside for 1/2 hour.

Put 8 cups water in a large steamer. Spread a damp cheesecloth over it, leaving the corners hanging out. Pour in batter and sprinkle beans over the batter. Push beans in lightly with a spoon. Cover steamer with lid, and steam for 45 minutes. Turn heat off and let sit for 5 minutes. Lift up a corner of the cheesecloth. If cornbread comes off then it is done. Take out and serve.

KOREAN STYLE RED BEAN AND FLOUR CAKE

2 1/2   cups flour
1/2   teaspoon salt (divided)
1   cup dried red beans (Oriental)
6   cups water (divided)

Slowly cook beans in 5 cups water for 45 minutes.   Add 1/4 teaspoon salt. Set side.

Mix flour and 1/4 teaspoon salt in a bowl. Slowly add 1 cup water. Knead. Let sit for 5 minutes.

Tear off balls a little bigger than walnut-size. Flatten to 1/2-inch thickness. Drop into sauce pan with beans. Boil. Turn heat down and cook for 10 minutes. Check. When there is no liquid left in the pan, it is done.

Put in a pie pan. Cook in oven at 350 degrees for 1/2 hour. Check tenderness. Serve.

STEAMED SWEET RICE CAKE WITH CHESTNUTS

3   cups sweet rice flour
2   cups rice flour
1/2   teaspoon salt
1   cup sugar
1   cup water (approximately)
2-3   cups fresh chestnuts, or 2 cups dried chestnuts
1   tablespoon sugar

Mix flours, salt and 1 cup sugar in a large bowl. Gradually add water and mix. Smooth out lumps by rubbing through hands. Then put through a sifter. When done, pinch powder and it should cling together.

In a separate bowl mix chestnuts and 1 tablespoon sugar. Set aside.

Put 8 cups water in steamer. Wet 2 cheesecloths and drape over pot, leaving corners hanging out. Put 2 1/2 cups of flour mixture on cheesecloths. Cover with chestnuts. Top with remaining flour.

Steam covered for approximately 1 1/2 hour. Serve.

STEAMED SWEET RICE CAKES
(SHAPED LIKE CLAMS)

1   **cup sweet rice flour**
5   **cups rice flour**
5   **cups water**
1   **teaspoon salt**
2   **cups sesame seeds, roasted**
1/4   **cup sugar**
6   **ounces pine needles**
1   **cup water**
1   **tablespoon sesame oil**

Mix flours and salt in a bowl. Gradually add water. Knead for approximately 1/2 hour.

Mix sesame seeds and sugar in a bowl. Make walnut size balls with dough. Flatten each ball and put 1 teaspoon of sesame seed filling on and close up.

Wash pine needles well with soap, rinse and dry. Put 8 cups water in a steamer. Wet 2 cheesecloths and drape over pot, leaving corners hanging out. Layer some rice cakes on cheesecloth. Top with pine needles, then with remaining rice cakes, and remaining pine needles.

Steam covered for approximately 45 minutes. Serve.

STEAMED SWEET RICE CAKE WITH PUMPKIN

3   **cups sweet rice flour**
2   **cups rice flour**
1/2   **teaspoon salt**
1 1/2 **cup sugar**
1   **cup water (approximately)**
2   **cups dried pumpkin**
1   **tablespoon sugar**

Mix flours, salt and sugar in a large bowl. Gradually add water and mix. Smooth out lumps by rubbing through hands. Then put through a sifter. When done, pinch powder and it should stick together.

In a separate bowl mix the dried pumpkin and 1 tablespoon sugar. Put 8 cups water in steamer. Wet 2 cheesecloths and drape over pot, leaving corners hanging out. Put 2 1/2 cups of flour mixture on cheesecloths. Cover with dried pumpkin. Top with remaining flour.

Steam covered for approximately 1 1/2 hours. Serve.

FRIED BUNS WITH BROWN SUGAR

1   **loaf prepared white bread dough**
1   **cup brown sugar (divided)**
1   **tablespoon oil**

Roll all the dough into 3 inch circles. Add 1/2 teaspoon of brown sugar or more if desired to each circle. Roll all the circles into balls. Fry till golden brown in about 1 tablespoon of oil. Serve.

Notes

Snacks

DRIED PERSIMMON

History: Eat only 1-2 persimmons at a time, because you might get sick. This is good medicine for stomach problems. For 5 generations my family has used this for medicine, and it works very well. My mother always gave it to me if I had stomach problems, and it worked well.

Bitter persimmon
Powdered sugar

Peel persimmon, then dry it. Make stem 1-2 inches long and tie a string onto it. Dry it in the sun. To test if dry enough, pinch in the middle, and it should be slightly soft.

Take the top off, and flatten persimmon to an inch of thickness. Then put on a plate, and sprinkle with white powder sugar. Dry as many as desired.

TURKEY JERKY

1	tablespoon liquid smoke
1	cup sugar
3	pounds turkey roast
3	green onions
1 1/2	cups soy sauce
1	tablespoon black pepper
2	tablespoons sesame oil
1	teaspoon garlic, chopped

Put turkey in a flat container. Mix rest of ingredients and pour over turkey. Mix. Smooth out over bottom of pan.

Must refrigerate for 2 days. Turn the meat over a few times during the marinating process.

Place the meat in a dehydrator and dry according to your machine's directions or to your desire. Serve.

KOREAN STYLE BEEF JERKY

2 pounds sirloin tip roast (remove excess fat and gristle)
5 tablespoons sugar
1 cup soy sauce
1 tablespoon garlic powder
2 tablespoons hickory liquid smoke
2 tablespoons black pepper
1 tablespoon sesame oil
1 tablespoon sesame seeds roasted and crushed
1 tablespoon powdered red pepper or flakes, use more for extra hot or less for real mild
2 green onions, minced
Dehydrator appliance

Slice beef about 1/8 inch thick.

To make marinade sauce put all ingredients together and mix. Put meat into bowl with the marinade sauce and stir or turn in meat so as to cover all the meat well with the sauce.

Marinate in sauce in refrigerator for 36 hours. Rotate and return for another 36 hours.

After the 3 days of marinating, put the meat in your dehydrator appliance. Dehydrate for 3 days. Switch tray positions after 1 and a 1/2 days to assure even drying. Vary time according to how your appliance functions. Dry well. Serve.

TURKEY BREAST JERKY

2 pounds boneless turkey breast, sliced
2 cups soy sauce
1 cup sugar, or to taste
1/2 teaspoon garlic powder
1 tablespoon liquid smoke
1 tablespoon sesame seeds (roasted)
1 tablespoon black pepper
3 green onions, minced

Cut bottoms off of green onions and wash, then mince. Slice turkey into 1/4-inch thick slices. Mix all ingredients except turkey in a flat container. Add sliced turkey and mix.

Refrigerate for 1 day. Turn the meat over a few times during the marinating process. Place the meat in the dehydrator and dry according to your machine's directions or your desire. Serve.

GINGER TURKEY JERKY

5 cups turkey breast
1 cup soy sauce
1/2 cup water
1/2 cup sugar
1 tablespoon chopped garlic
2 green onions, minced
1/2 teaspoon chopped ginger
1 tablespoon black pepper

Cut turkey breast into thin slices. Place into a container. Mix remaining ingredients in a bowl. Pour over turkey and mix.

Marinate for 3 days. Turn the meat every 5-6 hours. Place the meat in the dehydrator and dry according to your machine's directions or your desire. Serve.

DUCK JERKY

5   cups duck meat
1   cup soy sauce
1   tablespoon sesame seeds (roasted)
1   tablespoon garlic powder
1   tablespoon sesame oil
1   tablespoon black pepper
1   tablespoon liquid smoke
3   green onions, minced
1   cup sugar

Peel skin off duck. Slice lengthwise at an angle, into 1/4-inch thick slices. Mix with all ingredients. Cover in a bowl.

Let sit in refrigerator for 2 days. Turn the meat over a few times during the marinating process. The meat is now ready to dry.

Place meat in a dehydrator and dry according to your machine's directions or your desire. Serve.

SMOKED SALMON JERKY

2 1/2   pounds boneless salmon fillets
2   cups soy sauce
1/2   cup sugar
1   teaspoon garlic powder
1/2   cup White Zinfandel wine
1/2   teaspoon black pepper
1/8   cup sesame oil
1/4   cup sesame seeds (roasted)
3   green onions, chopped
1/8   cup smoke sauce

Wash and clean fish. Dab dry with a towel. Wash green onions and cut roots off. Chop. Mix all ingredients in a bowl. Let sit in refrigerator for 1 day, turning over once.

Place meat in a dehydrator and dry according to your machine's directions or your desire. Serve.

ROASTED PUMPKIN SEEDS

8   cups water
2   cups salt
2   cups pumpkin seeds

Mix all ingredients in a large bowl.

Let sit for two days at room temperature. Drain and roast in oven. Cook at 350 degrees for 10 minutes. Check. Serve.

Notes

Index

Beverages

Rice

Salads

Soups

Main Dishes

Snacks

Desserts